Unboxing Android USB

A Hands-On Approach with Real World Examples

Rajaram Regupathy

Apress

ISBN-13 (pbk): 978-1-4302-6208-4

ISBN-13 (electronic): 978-1-4302-6209-1

President and Publisher: Paul Manning
Lead Editor: Saswata Mishra
Technical Reviewers: Jan Axelson and Prathap Rajmohan
Editorial Board: Steve Anglin, Ewan Buckingham, Gary Cornell, Louise Corrigan, Jim DeWolf,
    Jonathan Gennick, Jonathan Hassell, Robert Hutchinson, Michelle Lowman,
    James Markham, Matthew Moodie, Jeff Olson, Jeffrey Pepper, Douglas Pundick,
    Ben Renow-Clarke, Dominic Shakeshaft, Gwenan Spearing, Matt Wade, Steve Weiss
Coordinating Editor: Mark Powers
Copy Editor: Kezia Endsley
Compositor: SPi Global
Indexer: SPi Global
Artist: SPi Global
Cover Designer: Anna Ishchenko

Distributed to the book trade worldwide by Springer Science+Business Media New York, 233 Spring Street, 6th Floor, New York, NY 10013. Phone 1-800-SPRINGER, fax (201) 348-4505, e-mail orders-ny@springer-sbm.com, or visit www.springeronline.com. Apress Media, LLC is a California LLC and the sole member (owner) is Springer Science + Business Media Finance Inc (SSBM Finance Inc). SSBM Finance Inc is a Delaware corporation.

For information on translations, please e-mail rights@apress.com, or visit www.apress.com.

Apress and friends of ED books may be purchased in bulk for academic, corporate, or promotional use. eBook versions and licenses are also available for most titles. For more information, reference our Special Bulk Sales–eBook Licensing web page at www.apress.com/bulk-sales.

Any source code or other supplementary material referenced by the author in this text is available to readers at www.apress.com/9781430262084. For detailed information about how to locate your book's source code, go to www.apress.com/source-code/.

To my father

Memories of the past
Remains in my heart
Those days were pleasant
But, still they cannot return

Now, I see my destination,
I ain't any incarnation
Need to work hard
To be on the right path
With god on my side
Hope to reach it with some pride.

—Rajaram

Contents at a Glance

About the Author xiii

About the Technical Reviewers xv

About the Contributor... xvii

Foreword xix

Acknowledgments xxi

Introduction xxiii

■Chapter 1: Getting Started: The Android USB Framework 1

■Chapter 2: Discovering and Managing USB Within Android 17

■Chapter 3: USB Storage 37

■Chapter 4: USB Tethering.. 69

■Chapter 5: USB Accessory 79

■Chapter 6: USB Audio 101

■Chapter 7: Android Debug Bridge (ADB) 125

■Appendix A: Battery Charging Using USB 139

■Appendix B: Using libusb in Android 157

Index 167

Contents

About the Author xiii

About the Technical Reviewers xv

About the Contributor xvii

Foreword xix

Acknowledgments xxi

Introduction xxiii

■Chapter 1: Getting Started: The Android USB Framework 1

Android CDD – USB 2

    USB Device Mode 2

    USB Host Mode 3

    USB Accessory Mode 4

Android USB Architecture 7

    USB Service 8

    USB Function 9

    android.hardware.usb 9

    Other Infra 9

    USB Service 11

    USB Function 11

libusbhost 11

Kernel USB File System 11

Other Infra 11

Android USB Packages 12

android.hardware.usb 12

UsbAccessory 12

UsbDevice 13

UsbManager 13

UsbDeviceConnection 13

UsbInterface 13

UsbEndpoint 14

UsbRequest 14

Conclusion 14

Chapter 2: Discovering and Managing USB Within Android 17

USB Device Management 18

USB Host Management 18

USB Service 18

USB Device Manager 21

USB Function Configuration 22

Android Gadget Driver uevents 24

USB Host Manager 27

Stage 1: Discovering a Device 29

Stage 2: Communicating with a Device 31

Stage 3: Terminating Communication with a Device 32

Sample 1: USBView 33

Conclusion 35

■Chapter 3: USB Storage 37

USB Mass Storage (UMS) Overview 39

Command Block Wrapper (CBW) 41

Command Status Wrapper (CSW) 41

Android Mass Storage Framework 43

Android USB Mass Storage Device Framework 43

Sharing the Storage 45

Android USB Mass Storage Host Framework 47

USB Media Transfer Protocol (MTP) Overview 49

Media Transfer Protocol Specification Overview 50

Android MTP Responder Framework 53

MTPServer 54

MTPRequestPacket 55

MTPResponsePacket 55

MTPDataPacket 55

MTPDatabase 55

MTPEventPacket 55

MTP Responder: Command/Response Sequence 56

Android MTP Initiator Framework 58

MTP Initiator: Discovering and Managing an MTP Device 60

Example 1: Switching MTP to UMS 62

Example 2: MTP Initiator Application 65

Conclusion 68

■Chapter 4: USB Tethering 69

RNDIS Specification Overview 71

Android USB Tethering Framework 74

Enabling USB Tethering 75

Example: Reverse Tethering Over USB 76

Design and Flow 77

Chapter 5: USB Accessory 79

Android Open Accessory Protocol 80

USB HID Specification 85

Android Open Accessory Framework 88

Conclusion 100

Chapter 6: USB Audio 101

USB Audio Specification 102

Android USB Audio 105

USB Host Audio 109

USB Device Audio 113

Conclusion 123

Chapter 7: Android Debug Bridge (ADB) 125

Setting Up ADB 127

Windows 127

Linux 128

ADB Protocol 128

Client <-> Server Protocol 129

Server <-> ADB Daemon Protocol 129

Android ADB Architecture 132

Example 1: Using JDB with ADB 135

Example 2: Backing Up Your Phone with ADB 136

Appendix A: Battery Charging Using USB 139

Types of USB Chargers 140

Wall Charger 140

Personal Computer 141

Charging Dock 141

USB Battery Specification Overview 142

Android Battery Charging Overview 146

Sample 1: Battery Status Explorer 152

　Design and Flo 152

Sample 2: Charging Completion Indicator 154

　Design and Flow 154

Conclusion 156

■Appendix B: Using libusb in Android 157

Overview of libusbhost 158

　USB Monitor 159

　USB Transfer Management 160

USB-Serial Driver Using libusb 160

Building and Installing the Package 162

Running the USB-Serial Application 163

Index 167

About the Author

Rajaram Regupathy has more than 15 years of professional experience in developing firmware and system software-embedded products. He enjoys designing and developing new technology products from scratch. He has patents in embedded domain and is also a senior ACM member. A Linux and open source enthusiast, he has published books on Linux USB stack programming and written numerous open source articles.

About the Technical Reviewers

Jan Axelson is the author of *USB Complete, USB Embedded Hosts*, and other books about hardware programming and design. Jan enjoys experimenting with computer interfaces, especially USB.

Prathap Rajmohan has 15 years of experience in embedded software development and has architected and developed embedded TCP/IPv4/IPv6 and USB stacks for VoIP phones and mobile devices. He is a Principal Software Engineer at Logitech, where he develops embedded firmware for Linux-based products. He holds a B.E. in Electronics and Communication from Anna University and an M.S. in Software Systems from BITS, Pilani.

About the Contributor

 **Sakethram Bommisetti** works as a Senior Software Engineer with Ericsson India and received his bachelor's degree in Engineering from NIT Nagpur. He has experience in porting different Android USB frameworks and Android USB kernel, and contributed to the development of examples in this book.

Foreword

Like millions of others around the world, I use Android every day. That's because Android is the OS that powers my phone.

Of course, Android isn't limited to phones; it's also popular in embedded systems of all kinds. And every phone or other Android device with a USB port needs programming to manage the USB communications.

When Rajaram Regupathy mentioned to me that he was thinking about writing a book on Android USB programming, I was delighted. I first encountered Rajaram in the USB Experts group he manages on LinkedIn. We discovered we were traveling parallel paths, exploring and writing about the USB universe from different perspectives. Although I'd been writing about USB hardware and programming for 15 years, Android USB programming was something I hadn't yet explored.

Now, writing a programming book is no easy task. You need the fortitude to pore over reams of documentation, the expertise to test and debug what the documents promise (sometimes the documents are wrong!), careful attention to include everything your readers need and nothing more, and an ability to present the information in a clear and logical way.

Rajaram was exactly the person for the job. If you need to program USB communications for Android, this book will put you on the road to success. I'm happy to add *Unboxing Android USB* to the short list of books that I recommend on USB technology.

Jan Axelson

Author of *USB Complete: The Developer's Guide and USB Embedded Hosts*

Acknowledgments

This is my second book and I look at it as a product that I have taken through various stages, from conceptualizing it, developing it, and finally realizing it. This book would not have been possible without collaboration and support by many people at various stages. I take this opportunity to thank them all.

First, I would like to thank my Acquisition Editor, Saswata Mishra, who played a key role from conceptualization to the production stages of this book, providing effective input and suggestions. I would also like to thank Mark Powers, my Coordinating Editor, who helped make the process completely easy.

Sincere thanks to Jan for her kindness in accepting my request to review the book, for taking the time to review it, and for sharing valuable comments from her experiences. I also thank Prathap for his critical review of the text.

Special thanks to Sakethram for helping me out by preparing the Android examples and also by providing critical inside information.

I also thank my colleagues at Cypress for helping to include the FX3-based examples. Last but not least, I thank my wife, my daughter, and others for making this journey yet again a smooth one.

Introduction

The Android open platform, which was introduced in 2007, is now in more than 50 million devices. The application store statistics show billions of downloads. It has literally conquered the mobile handset market, overtaking many established players. It is also expanding beyond mobile platforms into unique products such as the Android Stick, which converts a normal TV to a smart one.

If you are a developer who works on embedded systems, there is no escape from this ever-growing platform. This inevitability creates a need for good reference books for engineers who are interested in getting started with Android. There are many books in the market covering Android application programming and its development environment. If you are looking for something like that in this book, you are in the wrong place. This book is much more than that. The book explains the complete Android framework, from the API to the internals of Android, along with the kernel below them.

This book exclusively covers the internals of the Android USB framework. Why USB? Similar to the Android platform, USB is also inevitable in the embedded world. On the Android platform, USB is the primary connectivity solution, as an interface used to debug and also as an interface used to charge the batteries of the Android device.

Does this mean this book is only for USB engineers? In fact, it will be useful to any developer working on the Android platform. Why?

If you are a multimedia developer on the Android platform, you need USB for media transfer or to play back audio. This book explores MTP and USB audio in both USB device and USB host modes.

If you are a core developer who works on charging, you need to understand the USB charging specifications, which are explained in the book.

If you are a networking developer interested in tethering, USB plays a role using the RNDIS specification, which is explained in the book.

If you are an application developer interested in managing USB devices from an Android platform, this book explores the Android USB Service framework, which manages USB functionalities.

Last but not least, Android Debug Bridge (ADB), the debugging tool of Android, is over USB and knowledge of its internals is a definite value-add for any application or platform developer. This book details the internals of ABD to the kernel level.

This book covers everything about USB on Android, from the different USB classes supported in device mode to the USB host framework that manages the USB devices connected to the Android platform. Each chapter explains USB class specification before exploring how the functionality (class) is implemented on the Android platform. This gives readers a clean perspective as to what the USB specification demands and how it is implemented in Android.

The Android framework has migrated to different versions by now. As a platform or application developer, it's important you know about the major changes each version introduced. The book covers the major changes in the USB framework between the versions, including interesting bug fixes that were undocumented in the Android specifications.

Intended Audience

The primary audience for this book are application developers and engineers who work hands-on with Android. This book is for an application developer who has an idea for a USB app and wonders how to implement it. This book will be a definite guide for the developer to manage USB on Android.

Because the book covers APIs to the Linux kernel, core platform developers will find it easy to put data point to debug. Thus, core Android platform developers working on USB, audio, media, and others are the next primary audience for the book.

Technical managers, architects, and senior managers who look for the eagle-eye view of a system are a secondary audience for the book. The book will enable them to understand the different blocks of the Android USB subsystem and help estimate the complexity involved.

Student and engineers can use this book as a do-it-yourself reference, as it explains the different blocks of the Android USB framework, from the application level to the kernel.

What You'll Learn

Understand the Android USB framework, from the APIs to the kernel layer, and enable advanced USB application development.

Learn all the major USB functionalities by exploring the USB class specifications not covered in any of the USB books.

Learn the newly introduced Android Open Accessory (AOA) protocol and explore the developing NFC reader using the AOA protocol.

Learn about critical changes in the Android USB framework among different Android versions.

Learn how USB charging works, with an explanation of the USB battery specification.

Learn how to switch between MTP and mass storage and vice versa, in order to share storage with a host PC.

Salient Features

Real-world useful applications enhance your Android experience, including reverse tethering, AOA audio, AOA NFC reader, switching between MTP and UMS, and more. Complete project source is available, which will help you try it on your own.

Covers advanced technical topics (Android and USB) that aren't covered in other texts.

All design diagrams (Microsoft Visio) are on the CD for reuse by developers and architects.

Covers the major differences in the Android USB framework between Android versions.

Covers all major USB functions, such as MTP, audio, charging, and mass storage, along with Google-defined USB functions like ADB and AOA, all by exploring their specifications.

Chapter Introduction

Though there are different types of Android-powered devices, this book details the Android USB framework with a mobile hand-held device in mind. The following section provides a brief description of each chapter in this book.

Getting Started: The Android USB Framework

Android defines its requirement through the Compatibility Definition Document (CDD) and mandates that Android devices comply with this specification. This chapter provides a brief overview of the USB requirements defined in the Android CDD. The chapter subsequently explains various USB-related Android APIs that the Android framework exports for application developers in order to manage USB functionalities or devices.

Discovering and Managing USB Within Android

Discovering and managing a device is the first step and a crucial part any programming activity. This chapter describes how USB function discovery is made inside the Android framework when an Android device is connected in USB device mode. The chapter also details how a USB device is detected inside the Android framework when an Android device is connected in host mode.

USB Storage

Media is one of the key features of mobile devices and is predominantly managed using USB. Media over USB is managed using two USB specifications: Media Transfer Protocol (MTP) and Mass Storage Class (UMS). This chapter briefly details these two specifications and provides an overview of the USB specification's requirements. The chapter also details how media files are transferred to a host PC when the Android device is in USB device mode (both UMS and MTP).

This chapter also explains how a USB-based external media device (say, a USB flash drive or an MTP device) is managed by the Android framework in USB host mode.

USB Tethering

Tethering is a method by which mobile devices shares their Internet connectivity with other devices, such as personal computers or laptops. An Android device uses the RNDIS protocol over USB to tether and share Internet connectivity with other devices. The RNDIS protocol is Microsoft-specific and is very similar to the USB ECM class specification. This chapter provides a brief overview of the RNDIS specification and explains the USB part of the Android framework that facilitates tethering.

USB Accessory

Android Open Accessory (AOA), an Android-specific class defined by Google, was introduced in the Ice Cream Sandwich version of Android to facilitate Android devices in managing external devices. The chapter details the AOA protocol and its operations with an example application. With the Jelly Bean version of Android, the AOA protocol was improved to support the USB Human Interface Device (HID) class. The chapter provides a brief overview of the USB HID class and its implementation inside the Android framework.

USB Audio

The USB audio specification defines transport that provides an efficient way to propagate and control digital audio. With the Jelly Bean version of Android, an Android system in USB device mode supports the USB audio class. This support of digital audio over USB is packed with the AOA protocol. This chapter provides a brief overview of USB audio specification and subsequently explains the Android framework that implements the device audio class. The chapter explains the device and host audio implementations within the Android framework.

Android Debug Bridge

Android Debug Bridge (ADB) is a command-line client/server debug tool that allows you to communicate with an Android-powered device using USB as a transport. This chapter details the ADB protocol defined by Google and subsequently explains how the Android USB framework implements the ADB protocol.

Appendix A: Battery Charging Using USB

Most battery-powered hand-held devices use a USB port to generate power for charging the battery. Android-powered hand-held devices also use USB as the primary power source to charge the battery. This USB class is covered as part of this appendix since there is no real Android USB framework for battery management. This is because USB charging specification focuses on the charging current and other low-level details; there is no USB-level protocol. This chapter provides a brief overview of the USB charging specification and subsequently explains the USB part of the Android battery manager framework.

Appendix B: Using libusb in Android

Protocols like USB allow developers to write driver at user space to manage its functionality. The USB user space driver called libusb is available in almost all popular desktop operating systems. Since libusb is a generic driver, it can be used with any USB device. This chapter explores how to write a simple application over libusb on the Android platform.

## Chapter 1

Getting Started: The Android USB Framework

What you will learn:

- Android USB CDD requirements
- Overview of Android USB packages
- Architectural diagram of Android USB framework
- Android USB APIs

Android has become one of the most successful open platforms, powering up millions of mobile devices and similar embedded devices worldwide. According to Google, more than a million new Android devices are added to this statistic every day. This large market presence and continuous market penetration makes it the ideal platform for developers, SMEs, and bigger enterprises to portray their presence and reach out to end users. For Android devices, Google provides the necessary infrastructure to develop new applications. These devices can reach millions of end users through Google's open market platform named "Google Play."

Such a large development and deployment process necessitates standardization in order to ensure compatibility of these applications across the multitudes of Android devices that exist. To facilitate this, Google created a compatibility program that enables application developers, end users, and platform manufacturers to maintain program consistency and a similar user experience across devices. A detailed overview of the compatibility program is available on Google's Android web site at https://source.android.com/compatibility/overview.html. The compatibility program consists of three key components: Compatibility

Definition Document (CDD), Android Platform Source Code, and a Compatibility Test Suite (CTS). Any device that claims to be an "Android" device has to comply with the Android CDD and successfully pass all CTS test suites.

In order to study the framework within Android, it is important to understand the aforementioned three key components. Thus, in order to best study the Android USB framework, it is important to focus and explore what Android CDD defines as a USB requirement, and how that requirement is implemented.

This chapter starts with exploring the USB section of the Android CDD, and subsequently presents a complete overview of the Android USB framework by providing a break down of the implementation process. Later on, the chapter will explore various USB APIs that the Android framework exports in order to assist an application developer in managing the USB functionality of an Android device.

Android CDD – USB

At the time of this writing, Android 4.4 Kit Kat is the latest version of Android and Android 4.4 CDD defines the compatibility requirement of the Android Kit Kat version. You can find the complete list of Android CDDs on Google's Android website at http://source.android.com/compatibility/downloads.html. So, what is an Android CDD? In simple terms, the Android CDD defines the requirements that must be met in order for a device to claim that it is an Android-compatible device. To an extent, Android CDD is brief in that it is a 30-40 page document. This document can point to specifications like the USB Audio, for example, to indicate the user's expectation. The CDD also identifies features as "must," "must not," "required," "shall," "shall not," "should," "should not," "recommended," "may," and "optional," as per the IETF standard that is defined in RFC2119. It is important for developers to pay attention to these terms and take care while developing Android applications when using an optional feature or any feature listed as "may."

When it comes to USB, an Android device can operate in two modes—USB device mode or USB host mode.

USB Device Mode

When an Android device is connected to a host PC using USB, as illustrated in Figure 1-1, the Android device is said to be in USB device mode and power is sourced from the host PC USB port. (A device that needs more power than the host can provide should have its own power source.)

Figure 1-1. Illustration of an Android device in USB device mode

USB Host Mode

When a USB device is connected to an Android device, as illustrated in
Figure 1-2, the Android device is said to be in USB host mode, and the
Android device has to supply power to the connected device. An Android
device functioning as a USB embedded host or as an On-The-Go (OTG)
host must supply 5V/500mA of power when the connected device is USB
bus powered.

Figure 1-2. Illustration of an Android device in USB host mode

There is also a unique Android USB setup, which was introduced during the
Honeycomb version of Android, named the USB accessory mode.

USB Accessory Mode

In USB accessory mode, an Android device that is in the USB device mode can manage external devices. This ability is achieved by connecting the Android device to an external embedded accessory device, which acts as a USB host. The Android device goes to USB accessory mode in order to manage devices that connect to the accessory device. Figure 1-3 depicts Android accessory mode with a simple illustrative example of managing a camera from an Android device using an accessory device. Accessory mode is explained in detail in Chapter 5, which will provide you with a better understanding of the process.

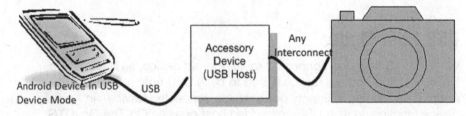

Figure 1-3. Illustration of an Android device in USB accessory mode

The USB section of Android CDD defines which USB functionalities have to be supported in the host and device modes. Tables 1-1 and 1-2 capture the requirements when an Android device acts as a USB device or as a USB host.

Table 1-1. Illustration of an Android CDD 4.4 as Defined in USB Device Requirements

USB Device Requirement

- The port must be connectable to a USB host with a standard USB-A port.

- The port should use the micro-USB form factor on the device side. Existing and new devices that run Android 4.4 are very strongly encouraged to meet these requirements in Android 4.4 so that they will be able to upgrade to future platform releases.

- The port should be centered in the middle of an edge. Device implementations should either locate the port on the bottom of the device (according to natural orientation) or enable software screen rotation for all apps (including the home screen), so that the display draws correctly when the device is oriented with the port at the bottom. Existing and new devices that run Android 4.4 are very strongly encouraged to meet these requirements in Android 4.4 so that they will be able to upgrade to future platform releases.

(continued)

Table 1-1. (continued)

USB Device Requirement

- If the device has other ports (such as a non-USB charging port) it should be on the same edge as the micro-USB port.

- It must allow a host connected to the device to access the contents of the shared storage volume using either USB Mass Storage Protocol or the Media Transfer Protocol.

- It must implement the Android Open Accessory API and specification as documented in the Android SDK documentation, and also must declare support for the hardware feature android.hardware.usb. accessory [Resources, 52].

- It must implement the USB audio class (version not mentioned in CDD) as documented in Android SDK documentation (http://developer. android.com/reference/android/hardware/usb/UsbConstants. html#USB_CLASS_AUDIO).

- It should implement support for USB battery charging specification (version 1.2) [Resources, 64]. Existing and new devices that run Android 4.4 are very strongly encouraged to meet these requirements in Android 4.4, so that they will be able to upgrade to future platform releases.

- Device implementations must implement the Android Debug Bridge. If a device implementation omits a USB client port, it must then implement the Android Debug Bridge via a local area network (such as Ethernet or 802.11).

Table 1-2. Illustration of an Android CDD 4.4 as Defined in USB Host Requirements

USB Host Requirement

- It may use a non-standard port form factor, but if so, the device must be shipped with a cable or cables that will adapt the port to a standard USB-A.

- It must implement the Android USB host API as documented in the Android SDK and declare support for the hardware feature android.hardware.usb.host (http://developer.android.com/guide/ topics/usb/host.html).

These requirements are defined in section 7.7 USB of the Android CDD 4.4, and you should also note that the requirements are brief and point to the actual specifications. It is important to note that there are few requirements that define actual physical characteristics of an Android device. These physical characteristics will be handy when maintaining compatibility with external accessories, such as audio docks.

Over and above these two tables, USB requirements can also be found across other sections such as "Memory and Storage." The following snippet captures one such requirement from the storage section of CDD:

"Regardless of the form of shared storage used, device implementations MUST provide some mechanism to access the contents of shared storage from a host computer, such as USB mass storage (UMS) or Media Transfer Protocol (MTP). Device implementations MAY use USB mass storage, but SHOULD use Media Transfer Protocol. If the device implementation supports Media Transfer Protocol:

- The device implementation should be compatible with the reference Android MTP host and Android File Transfer [Resources, 57].

- The device implementation should report a USB device class of 0x00.

- The device implementation should report a USB interface name of MTP.

If the device implementation lacks USB ports, it must then provide a host computer with access to the contents of the shared storage by some other means, such as a network file system."

The storage section defines how the storage space of an Android device should be shared by a host PC over USB. The storage section explains in detail mandating MTP as the preferred USB protocol for sharing the storage space.

 DID YOU KNOW?

Have you ever wondered why your Android device is not enumerating as Mass Storage device from Ice Cream Sandwich and later? The secret lies in Android CDD. From the following two snippets, it is very apparent that Android has moved from Mass Storage to MTP as the default mechanism to connect to the host computer.

Android CDD 2.3 – Ginger Bread Version

"It must implement the USB mass storage specification, to allow a host connected to the device to access the contents of the /sdcard volume."

Android CDD 4.0.3 – Ice Cream Sandwich Version

"Regardless of the form of shared storage used, device implementations MUST provide some mechanism to access the contents of shared storage from a host computer, such as USB mass storage (UMS) or Media Transfer Protocol (MTP). Device implementations may use USB mass storage, but should use Media Transfer Protocol."

Now that you are able to understand Google Android's USB requirements, you can now explore how these requirements are built within the Android framework.

Android USB Architecture

This section explains Android USB architecture based on the various USB modes in which an Android device can perform as explained in the initial section. In simple terms, an Android platform is made of Android Linux kernel as the base to manage the platform resources. A Java-based Android framework sits on top of Android Linux kernel, providing the necessary user experience. Some Android features lay within the kernel, and certain features are available only at the Android framework. In case of USB, the functionality is managed between the Android Linux kernel and the user space Android framework.

 DID YOU KNOW?

An important point to note is that the kernel discussed here is called the "Android Linux kernel" because it's not same as the generic Linux kernel, and most importantly, not the same as the Linux USB gadget framework. The USB device stack is referred to as the USB gadget framework, and is yet to be integrated as part of the mainline kernel.

The following section provides a top-level architectural view of Android USB in USB device mode, detailing the complete Android USB starting from the Android Linux kernel to the user space Android framework.

When you connect an Android device to a host PC, the Android device is said to be in USB device mode and can export multiple USB functionalities like MTP, ADB, or CDC to the host PC through its descriptors. This type of USB device is referred as a composite device, where a single USB device supports multiple USB functions through their interfaces. From the architecture diagram shown in Figure 1-4, you can infer that the composite infrastructure is part of the kernel and most of the USB device functions are implemented as "class drivers" within the Android Linux kernel. There are exceptions, like ADB and MTP, which are implemented on both sides, i.e. the kernel and user space. In such cases, the kernel driver implements just the transport part of USB, guaranteeing delivery of the data. The Android framework performs the functional management, implementing the class-level protocol, which other chapters of this book will explore in more detail later. The following section provides a brief overview of the architectural blocks used in the USB device mode, as represented in Figure 1-4.

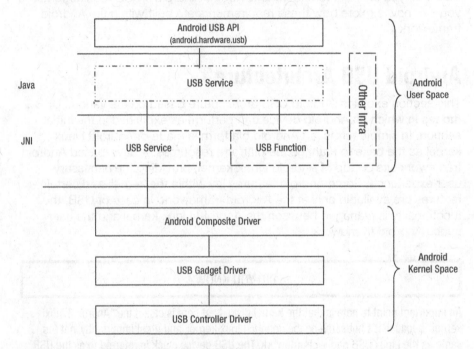

Figure 1-4. Android USB device framework architecture

USB Service

The USB Service framework is the key factor and is the backbone in Android USB device mode. In a way, the role of this framework is to listen to and communicate state changes in Android kernel USB driver and subsequently pass that information on to other interested Android frameworks. Those frameworks then pass that information further to other modules by broadcasting their intent with only the necessary information. This framework also manages USB functions that an Android device has to share when connected to a host PC. More details about this framework will be explained further in Chapter 2, entitled "Discovering and Managing USB within Android."

USB Function

Most of the USB functions are implemented in the Android Linux kernel space. However, USB functions like ADB or MTP are implemented as user space daemons integrated within the Android framework. This block represents the daemons that implement USB Class requirements. Subsequent chapters on ADB and MTP provide a detailed view on how this module interacts with the kernel below and other Android frameworks.

android.hardware.usb

Android APIs for USBs are represented as a android.hardware.usb package and are discussed in further detail in later sections of this chapter. In a USB device mode, these APIs have a minimal role, as there are no APIs that allow managing a USB device's functionality. The exception to this is Android accessory mode, where developers are required to write applications to manage external devices over USB device mode.

Other Infra

Within the Android framework there are many other frameworks that are interested in the USB state changes, like connection, disconnection, or a switch of USB functionalities. This "other infra" represents Android modules like storage infrastructure, network daemon infrastructure, and charging infrastructure, to name a few that are interested in USB state changes. These other infrastructures hook themselves up to the USB framework for the *Intent* that the USB Service module generate. In Chapter 2, we will provide some insight into how to listen to USB states changes. Other chapters will deal with storage and tethering, including details of how they hook and receive the necessary information.

This module also represents the user interface part of Android that communicates USB state changes to the user over the Notification panel. The Android USB architecture is the same in USB accessory mode and USB device mode, as accessory mode is nothing but the USB device mode with some deviation.

Now that you understand how the Android framework in USB device mode works, you can explore the Android framework in USB host mode. Similar to device mode, host mode keeps most of the class functions implemented within the Linux kernel, but classes like MTP host mode are implemented in Android user space. It is important to note that, unlike the device stack (gadget driver), which differs from the mainline Linux kernel, the USB host stack is same as the mainline Linux kernel. Though Linux kernel has support for almost all USB devices, an Android device in USB host mode might not support all devices because the Android device is functioning as a limited capability USB embedded host or USB OTG host. It is important to note that Android CDD did not define USB host functionalities like it did for the USB device mode. Thus USB host class support, like support for the 3G dongle, is determined by the Android device manufacturer.

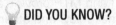 **DID YOU KNOW?**

A PC host can support most of the USB devices in the market, but a USB OTG host or USB-embedded host typically supports a much smaller set of devices. A USB OTG host or a USB embedded host provides a list of supported devices called the Targeted Peripheral List (TPL) and presents only those devices to the user. According to the USB On-The-Go and Embedded Host specification, it is unreasonable for an OTG host or embedded host to support all range of USB devices. For example, connecting a camera to a printer may make sense, but it does not make sense for a printer to support a USB barcode scanner or a USB speaker.

Figure 1-5 provides a top-level architecture diagram of the Android USB host mode framework.

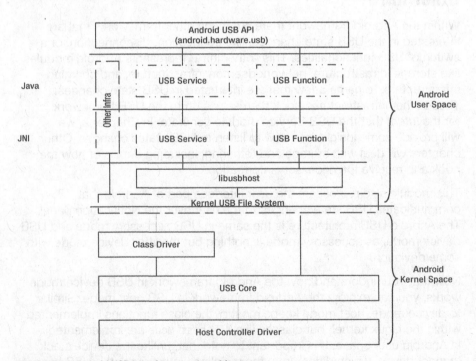

Figure 1-5. Android USB host framework architecture

USB Service

Similar to device mode, USB Service is the key part in the USB host mode. The main role of this framework is to detect state changes like connection and disconnection within the USB host kernel drivers, and convert those changes into a format that is understood in the Android space. This framework is explained in greater detail in Chapter 2.

USB Function

USB host mode classes (functions) like MTP are implemented within the Android framework, and their functionality is spread across the Java and JNI layers. This USB function framework represents the class implementation and the implementation necessary for USB Host APIs. Thus, the main role of this framework is to translate USB application requests and communicate them to the USB device connected to the kernel below. Chapter 3, "USB Storage," provides a detailed picture of USB function implementation while Chapter 2 provides internals of USB Host APIs.

libusbhost

One of the most popular USB user space drivers on Linux is libusb, while libusbhost is a similar, thinner version of it, adapted to Android USB host requirements. The main role of this library is to act as an interface between the Linux kernel USB driver and the Android USB framework. This also makes it possible to implement necessary infrastructure to facilitate detection of any new USB device connected to the kernel below. A more detailed analysis of libusbhost is available as part of Appendix B, "Using libusb in Android." Chapter 3, "USB Storage," and Chapter 2 also provide detail about how the library is used within the Android USB framework.

Kernel USB File System

In USB host mode, the kernel file system plays a key role, starting from detecting a USB device when it gets identified within the kernel, to transferring information from Android to the kernel space. To better understand the USB host mode operation, it is important to first understand the kernel USB file system.

Other Infra

Inside the Android framework, there are other frameworks like audio, volume daemon, and so on, that are interested in knowing USB state changes. Some of these infrastructures take on the role of presenting the USB functionality to the user.

Having understood the Android USB requirements and the top-level blocks of Android USB framework, you'll now explore the various USB-related APIs that the Android framework exposes in order to manage a USB device or functionality.

Android USB Packages

The Android framework is a Java-based system, and the term "package" is used in Java programming to organize similar Java classes into a namespace. This practice enables programmers to easily manage access rights and avoid conflicts. Along the same line of thought, Android USB functional implementations are collated in a single namespace, called the android.hardware.usb. This section explores different USB classes collated in this package, as well as the APIs that deliver these USB classes' exports to a programmer. The section further covers the MTP class, a USB host function packaged separately to manage media device connected to an Android device over USB.

android.hardware.usb

The android.hardware.usb package is a collection of USB host APIs and USB accessory APIs. USB host APIs were introduced as part of Android Honey Comb 3.1 version (API level 12), and the support is available on Android 3.1 and higher. USB accessory APIs were introduced in Android Honey Comb 3.1 version (API level 12) as well, but the support was back-ported to Android Ginger Bread 2.3.4 version (API level 10). The back-ported version of accessory APIs can be imported using the package name com.android.future.usb. The next sections explore the different classes and their functions.

UsbAccessory

This class represents a USB accessory device connected to an Android device that's in USB device mode. Note that a USB accessory is an external hardware device acting as a USB host, as explained in Figure 1-3.

When an accessory device is connected to an Android device, applications can search for and get product information like the manufacturer name, model, version, and so on, from other devices that connect to the accessory. This class provides necessary methods for an application developer to get product information, as previously stated. Complete details of this class are available at http://developer.android.com/reference/android/hardware/usb/UsbAccessory.html. A detailed analysis of how these accessory methods work is explained in detail in Chapter 5, "Android Accessory."

UsbDevice

This class represents a USB device connected to an Android in USB host mode. A UsbDevice object contains information that describes the capabilities and other USB specific details of the USB device, such as protocol, class, device ID, and so on. It is important to note that a UsbDevice can be instantiated by a UsbService implementation of the UsbHostManager. Complete details of this class are available at http://developer.android.com/reference/android/hardware/usb/UsbDevice.html.

UsbManager

This class is the core part of the Android USB package. It provides the state information of USB and discusses the methods to communicate with the USB devices that are connected. At this moment of writing, this class provides methods only for host mode. The class provides the necessary methods in order to provide permission to the USB device and shares the intent that communicates state information. Complete details of this class are available at http://developer.android.com/reference/android/hardware/usb/UsbManager.html.

UsbDeviceConnection

This class is used to provide the necessary methods for the user to send and receive data to a USB device. An instance of the usefulness of this class is when an application opens a USB device using the openDevice method. This class supports the transfer of bulk and controls data synchronously, unlike the queue method of UsbRequest. It also provides the requestWait method, which is used for asynchronous data transfer. Complete details of this class are available at http://developer.android.com/reference/android/hardware/usb/UsbDeviceConnection.html.

UsbInterface

This class is also used to represent an interface of a USB device connected to the Android host. An interface in USB is used to represent functionalities of the USB device. If a USB device has multiple functionalities, there will be multiple UsbInterface objects. This class provides methods to retrieve class, protocol, and endpoint details. Complete details of this class are available at http://developer.android.com/reference/android/hardware/usb/UsbInterface.html.

UsbEndpoint

This class is used to represent the endpoint of an interface and provides methods that can retrieve the details of an endpoint. In USB terms, this class provides information from a USB endpoint descriptor of a connected device. At the time of this writing, there is no support for an isochronous endpoint. Complete details of this class are available at http://developer. android.com/reference/android/hardware/usb/UsbEndpoint.html

UsbRequest

This class represents a USB packet used to read and write to or from a connected USB device. An object of UsbRequest is used to transfer bulk or to interrupt data asynchronously. After "queuing" a request, a program has to wait for the response using the requestWait method of UsbDeviceConnection. This class does not support control transfer over endpoint zero. At the time of this writing, support for isochronous transfer has not been provided. Complete details of this class are available at http://developer.android.com/reference/android/hardware/usb/ UsbRequest.html.

These classes discussed previously, other than UsbAccessory, constitute the Android USB host APIs and are packaged as android.hardware.usb.host for developers who create USB host applications. There are other packages, like android.mtp, that are derived from these set of APIs. The android. mtp class provides MTP class support for an application developer, and a detailed analysis of this process is provided in Chapter 3, "USB Storage."

Conclusion

Android is widely deployed across many platforms and different vendors, and it is important to have interoperability and to maintain quality. Android defines a brief requirement specification, namely the Android Compatibility Definition Document (CDD), to ensure that the different vendors of an Android device can interoperate easily. This chapter provided a brief overview of the USB requirements as defined in the latest Android CDD 4.4. This is applicable to the Jelly Bean version of Android. As discussed in this chapter, there have been few changes in the USB requirement, and you can explore different CDD versions to understand how USB requirements have evolved.

After discussing the CDD, this chapter also covered an architectural view of the Android USB framework. Subsequent chapters will explore each block of the Android USB framework in depth, and will cover their implementation with examples. As part of an Android USB introduction, this chapter also detailed different USB packages available for application developers to manage USB functionality on Android. The packages include classes that help manage the USB host and USB device functionality. A detailed analysis of these classes will be carried out in subsequent chapters.

Chapter **2**

Discovering and Managing USB Within Android

What you will learn:

- USB Service
- USB Device Manager
  - Architecture and Design Flow
  - Example Application – USB Functionality Viewer
- USB Host Manager
  - Architecture and Design Flow
  - Example Application – USBView
- Conclusion

An important first step in managing a device or resource is to detect and identify the device or resource from the system. This is the first step at the start of the program. To detect a resource, programs generally adapt mechanisms like polling, interrupt, or event, and then get to know the availability. Once a device or resource is detected and available, the program will try to take control of the resource to manage it. Similarly, Android USB framework has to provide mechanisms to detect or manage a USB device in USB host mode and detect or manage USB functionalities supported in USB device mode. This chapter introduces how Android USB frameworks identify a USB device or USB functionality, and covers the Linux kernel driver framework through the Android framework.

An Android device can be in USB device mode or USB host mode, thus requiring two different frameworks for detection, and the management of this is described in the following sections.

USB Device Management

When an Android device is connected to a PC via a USB port, USB functions (like ADB and mass storage) are enabled within the Android USB framework, and the Android device shows these functionalities in the PC. The process detecting a USB connection to a PC starts at the kernel, which subsequently communicates with the Android framework, which in turn, decides what USB function should be shared with the PC. The initial sections of this chapter explore this USB device detection process along with the framework that manages the USB device function.

USB Host Management

With more powerful application processors emerging in the market, mobile devices have started to support USB host mode operations. This means that users can now connect USB devices such as mice, keyboards, and USB flash drives, to their mobile devices. With Android running on such devices, it has to be able to detect those USB device connections and manage them. The later sections of this chapter explore how these USB devices are detected and managed by the Android framework when working as a USB host.

Within the Android framework, both of these management frameworks are part of a single framework called the *USB Service,* which acts as a control center for all other USB frameworks. This chapter explores the USB Service framework by providing a top-level view of the program's architecture initially, and then subsequently, explores the two key USB management frameworks in detail.

USB Service

USB Service is the core of the Android USB framework and is invoked as part of the Android System Server framework. The Android system server, which starts all the system services, starts the USB Service along with other services during boot up.

The implementation of starting UsbService is in frameworks/base/services/
java/com/android/server/SystemServer.java, as shown in the following
snippet.

```
try {
  Slog.i(TAG, "USB Service");
  // Manage USB host and device support
  usb = new UsbService(context);
  ServiceManager.addService(Context.USB_SERVICE, usb);
} catch (Throwabsle e) {
  reportWtf("starting UsbService", e);
}
```

Figure 2-1 illustrates how a USB Service framework is placed within the
Android USB framework, and how it acts as the central node of the Android
USB framework.

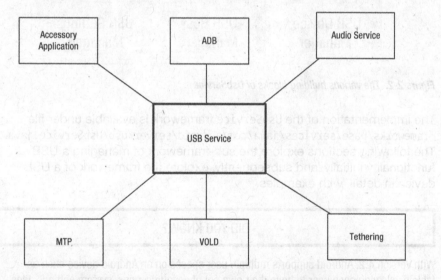

Figure 2-1. The USB Service framework acting as the core of USB functionality

Because the UsbService is the core, it's important that you understand
the internals of the UsbService framework. The UsbService framework
constitutes all USB related states, functionality, and communication of both
the host and device. The UsbService framework also includes permissions
and the setting framework, namely UsbSettingsManager, allowing control of
USB functionality within the Android framework.

As discussed in the previous chapter, USB functionality is managed through APIs exported via the package android.hardware.usb. Whenever an application invokes these USB APIs to either to manage USB functionality, or to manage a USB device the control is routed to the UsbService framework. The UsbService framework implements two sub-frameworks—the UsbDeviceManager and UsbHostManager frameworks. Whenever a host-related API call or event occurs, it is delegated to UsbHostManager, and when device events occur, control is delegated to UsbDeviceManager. Figure 2-2 illustrates the building blocks of the UsbService framework.

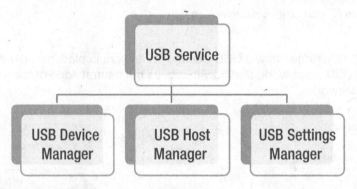

Figure 2-2. The various building blocks of UsbService

The implementation of the UsbService framework is available under file frameworks/base/services/java/com/android/server/usb/UsbService.java. The following sections explore the sub-framework of managing a USB functionality initially, and subsequently, explore the framework of a USB device in detail, with examples.

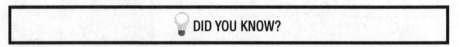

DID YOU KNOW?

With Version 4.2, Android supports multiple user spaces on an Android device such as tablets, allowing each user to have their own set of accounts, apps, system settings, files, and any other user-associated data. USB also supports this feature of having multiple user spaces, and is managed by the UsbService framework. The change is available through the following Change-Id, I8a723ad3d55ac1bff99276c5f3a3f5e8f013432f, and could help in understanding how the multiuser framework is implemented.

USB Device Manager

The USB Device Manager framework provides necessary functionalities to manage USB states when the Android device is in USB device mode. The framework is implemented in two files, namely /frameworks/base/ services/java/com/android/server/usb/UsbDeviceManager.java and frameworks/base/services/jni/com_android_server_UsbDeviceManager.cpp. The JNI implementation mostly takes care of the Android accessory class, which is detailed in subsequent chapters, and plays a very small role in managing the functionalities of the Android as a USB device. Android USB device functionality is mostly managed by the Java class framework UsbDeviceManager. Figure 2-3 illustrates a top-level view of UsbDeviceManager.

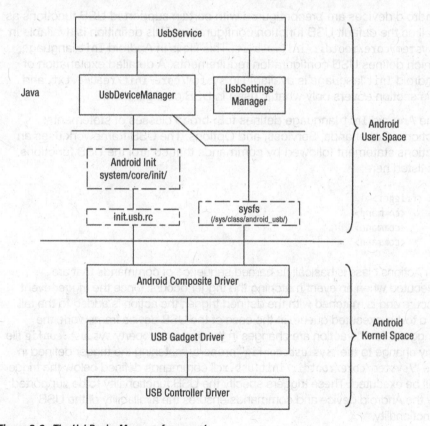

Figure 2-3. The UsbDeviceManager framework

Note that Figure 2-3 represents the UsbDeviceManager framework in a typical setup, without Android accessory functionality. That is the reason UsbDeviceManager JNI is not represented, as the role of the JNI is used only in Android accessory mode.

The UsbDeviceManager framework functionality can be visualized in two different sub-functionalities. One functionality listens for USB state changes when the Android device is in USB device mode, and the other manages the USB functionality in USB device mode. The following sections discuss how these two functionalities are implemented, and then subsequently explain them with control flow diagrams.

USB Function Configuration

Android devices are preconfigured with certain supported USB functions as well as the default USB function configuration. This definition is available in /system/core/rootdir/init.usb.rc. This file is in Android Init language, which defines USB configuration requirements. A detailed explanation of Android Init language is available in system/core/init/readme.txt, and this section covers only what is used in USB configuration.

The Android Init language defines four broad classes of statements: Actions, Commands, Services, and Options. The USB framework uses an Actions statement followed by commands that control the USB functions, as listed here:

```
on <trigger>
    <command>
    <command>
    <command>
```

An Actions class is basically a named sequence of commands that are executed when an event matching the trigger occurs. Once the trigger event occurs and is matched with the defined trigger, the action is added to the tail of a to-be-executed queue. In the case of the USB device framework, the "triggers" for the action are changes in the system property sys.usb.config file. Any change to the "sys.usb.config" property matching the trigger defined in the "/system/core/rootdir/init.usb.rc" commands defined below the trigger will be executed. These triggers specify the USB functionality to be supported by the Android device and commands ensures the availability of the USB functionality.

You may wonder how these functionalities are controlled. As you can infer from Figure 2-3, the Android gadget driver configurations are exported as files to the system directory named /sys/class/android_usb/. The parameters include the following list:

```
/sys/class/android_usb/android0/enable - Parameter that enables/disables
Android gadget driver
/sys/class/android_usb/android0/idVendor - Parameter used to send Android
devices vendor ID
/sys/class/android_usb/android0/idProduct  - Parameter used to send Android
devices product ID
/sys/class/android_usb/android0/functions – Used to set USB functions to be
supported by the Android gadget framework.
```

There are other functionality-specific parameters, which are discussed in the appropriate chapters to follow. During boot, these configurations are managed by init daemons implemented in /system/core/init/ that read, parse, and maintain·the list for subsequent use during system configuration.

Consider the following configuration from the init.usb.rc file, which handles ADB-only USB configuration:

```
# adb only USB configuration
# This should only be used during device bringup
# This should also only be used as a fallback if the USB
# manager fails to set a standard configuration
on property:sys.usb.config=adb
        write /sys/class/android_usb/android0/enable 0
            write /sys/class/android_usb/android0/idVendor 18d1
            write /sys/class/android_usb/android0/idProduct D002
            write /sys/class/android_usb/android0/functions ${sys.usb.config}
            write /sys/class/android_usb/android0/enable 1
            start adbd
            setprop sys.usb.state ${sys.usb.config}
```

In this action, when some Android framework sets the system property sys.usb.config to adb, Android disables the Android gadget framework(write /sys/class/android_usb/android0/enable 0), sets the VID/PID, and then sets the USB function to be supported. After the USB function to be supported is set, the control will back to the Android gadget framework(write /sys/class/android_usb/android0/enable 1). Since the enabled functionality is ADB, the 'adbd' daemon is then started. The command in the Actions class also sets the system property sys.usb.state to adb to indicate the UsbDeviceManager so that the transition of the function is completed. The section entitled "Case 2: Managing USB Device Mode Functionality," provides a detailed control flow of the USB function transition process.

Android Gadget Driver uevents

Linux kernel 2.6.10 (and onward) introduced a notification mechanism for kernel and user space communication called the uevent. Linux kernel uses Netlink to send kernel uevents to the user space. Netlink is a socket=like mechanism used in Linux to pass information between the kernel and the user process. Netlink, similar to a generic BSD socket infrastructure, supports primitive APIs like socket(), bind(), sendmsg(), and recvmsg(). Figure 2-4 provides a simple illustration of a uevent mechanism.

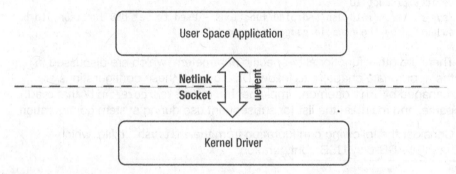

Figure 2-4. A simple representation of a uevent mechanism

These user events (uevents) that are generated from a kernel driver are used by user space daemons to create or remove device files, run programs, and load or remove a driver in the user land. These uevents are generally used to represent the lifecycle of a *kobject*, which is a data structure generally representing a device, to the user space.

The Android gadget kernel framework uses these uevents to communicate device states to the user space via the Android UsbDeviceManager framework. UsbDeviceManager listens to these uevents, collects and parses them, and then switches to the appropriate state. Within the kernel, the Android work function of the drivers/usb/gadget/android.c file implements the Android gadget driver. This gadget driver forms three different state strings with the keyword USB_STATE, in one of the formats shown here.

```
--cut--
char *disconnected[2] = { "USB_STATE=DISCONNECTED", NULL };
    char *connected[2]   = { "USB_STATE=CONNECTED", NULL };
    char *configured[2]  = { "USB_STATE=CONFIGURED", NULL };
    char **uevent_envp = NULL;
--cut--
```

When an Android device is connected as a USB device, the state of the device is checked from the gadget driver's flags. and the appropriate environmental data is assigned to the uevent_envp variable. For example, when the device is connected to the PC, USB_STATE=CONNECTED is set and when drivers are installed successfully and the device is functional, USB_STATE=CONFIGURED is set.

```
--cut--
        if (cdev->config)
                uevent_envp = configured;
        else if (dev->connected != dev->sw_connected)
                uevent_envp = dev->connected ? connected : disconnected;
--cut-
```

This state of information is then propagated to the user space using kobject_uevent_env, using the KOBJ_CHANGE action, as shown here.
```
--cut-

        if (uevent_envp) {
                kobject_uevent_env(&dev->dev->kobj, KOBJ_CHANGE, uevent_envp);
                pr_info("%s: sent uevent %s\n", __func__, uevent_envp[0]);
--cut-
```

In the user space, Android's UsbDeviceManager collects this USB_STATE information and broadcasts it to other frameworks that are interested in knowing the state change. Having an understanding of how the Android kernel passes information and how USB configurations are decided, you can now explore how UsbDeviceManager uses these frameworks to manage the USB device functionality of an Android device.

Case 1: Discovering USB Device State Changes

The process of managing USB functions within the Android UsbDeviceManager framework registers a uevent observer that will wait for state changes.

```
        // Watch for USB configuration changes
        mUEventObserver.startObserving(USB_STATE_MATCH);
```

USB_STATE_MATCH is defined as follows:

```
  private static final String USB_STATE_MATCH =
      "DEVPATH=/devices/virtual/android_usb/android0";
```

This string is used by the uevent observer to match the pattern in the string of uevents broadcasted by the kernel driver. Once the pattern matches the equivalent observer callback, in the UsbDeviceManager class is called. UsbDeviceManager then posts a message indicating that the USB state has changed, along with the state string (connected, disconnected, or configured). Figure 2-5 illustrates how UsbDeviceManager posts the message and then its subsequent actions.

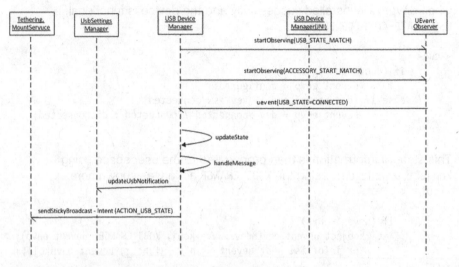

Figure 2-5. *The communication process during a connected uevent*

Case 2: Managing USB Device Mode Functionality

Once a state message is received, the next step is to set the USB configurations based on that state. The configuration setting is achieved by using setCurrentFunction. This internally sets the system property sys.usb.config with the current functions. As discussed in the previous section, this change in the system property will trigger a set of actions defined in the init.usb.rc file, thus enabling the Android device to switch to the particular USB function. Figure 2-6 shows the control flow when a user enables tethering that sets RNDIS as a USB function.

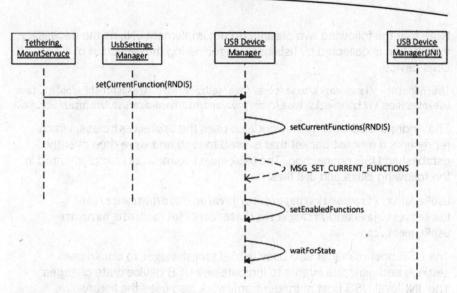

Figure 2-6. Managing USB functions

USB Host Manager

The USB host manager framework provides the necessary functionalities to manage the USB state when an Android device is in USB host mode and subsequently manages the USB device. Implementation of the USB host manager framework is spread across two files: `frameworks/base/services/java/com/android/server/usb/UsbHostManager.java` and `/frameworks/base/services/jni/com_android_server_UsbHostManager.cpp`. Internally, UsbHostManager provides the necessary framework to detect connections, disconnections, and opening of any USB device to the Android system. These functionalities are exported via UsbManager, a class of the `android.hardware.usb` package, as implemented in `/frameworks/base/core/java/android/hardware/usb/UsbManager.java`. The framework also collects information related to the connected USB device and shares them with the classes listed here, which help the classes interact with the USB device.

UsbDevice - /frameworks/base/core/java/android/hardware/usb/UsbDevice.java and frameworks/base/core/jni/android_hardware_UsbDevice.cpp
UsbDeviceConnection - /frameworks/base/core/java/android/hardware/usb/UsbDeviceConnection.java and /frameworks/base/core/jni/android_hardware_UsbDeviceConnection.cpp

Note that the following two classes do not implement JNI, as the necessary information is collected by UsbHostManager during the detection of a USB device.

UsbEndpoint- /frameworks/base/core/java/android/hardware/usb/UsbEndpoint.java
UsbInterface - /frameworks/base/core/java/android/hardware/usb/UsbInterface.java

The Android USB host framework also uses the UsbRequest class, which represents a request packet that is used to read and write data over the established USB connection. The UsbRequest framework is implemented in the following class and JNI files:

UsbRequest: /frameworks/base/core/java/android/hardware/usb/
UsbRequest.java and /frameworks/base/core/jni/android_hardware_
UsbRequest.cpp

The USB host manager also uses UsbSettingsManager to obtain user settings and generate intents to indicate any USB device state changes. The JNI-level USB host manager framework also uses the library libusbhost, which is implemented in /system/core/libusbhost/usbhost.c to interact with the Android kernel.

Figure 2-7 provides a brief overview of the UsbHostManager framework and its blocks, including the Android kernel USB blocks.

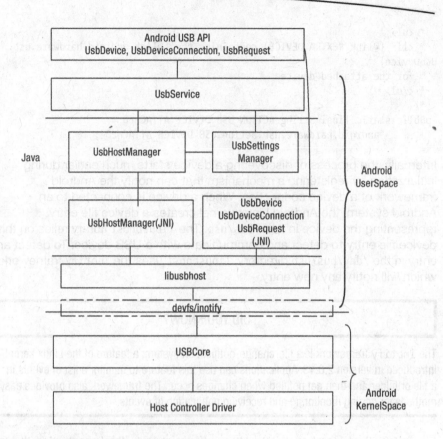

Figure 2-7. The UsbHostManager framework

Having seen the various blocks of the UsbHostManager framework, you can now learn how these blocks play a role in managing a USB device connected to the system. To do this, you'll classify the complete process into three stages: i) discovering a device, ii) communicating with a device, and iii) terminating communication with a device.

Stage 1: Discovering a Device

Discovery of a USB device that is being connected to an Android device at an application level is through the ACTION_USB_DEVICE_ATTACHED intent, as defined in Intent.java, listed here:

```
/**
 * Broadcast Action:  A broadcast for a USB device attached event.
 *
 * This intent is sent when a USB device is attached to the USB
 * bus when in host mode.
```

```
 * <ul>
 * <li> {@link #EXTRA_DEVICE} containing the {@link android.hardware.usb.
UsbDevice}
 * for the attached device
 * </ul>
 */
public static final String ACTION_USB_DEVICE_ATTACHED =
        "android.hardware.usb.action.USB_DEVICE_ATTACHED";
```

Internally, the process of discovering a device starts much earlier during initialization by registering a mechanism that can notify the Android framework of a device connection. When a device is connected to an Android system, the Android Linux kernel creates a device file entry representing the device in /dev/bus/usb. The libusbhost library relies on this device file entry to detect and communicate with a USB device. To detect an entry in the /dev/bus/usb directory, libusbhost uses the inotify framework, which will notify any new entry.

 DID YOU KNOW?

The inotify framework is a file-change-notification system, a feature of the Linux kernel introduced in version 2.6.13. Applications can use this feature to monitor a list of events in a file or folder and then get notified when changes occur. The framework also provides easy methods for adding monitoring and receiving notification of events.

Figure 2-8 illustrates how UsbHostManager registers to the kernel using the libusbhost library to detect a device and subsequently generate the ACTION_USB_DEVICE_ATTACHED intent using the UsbSettingsManager.

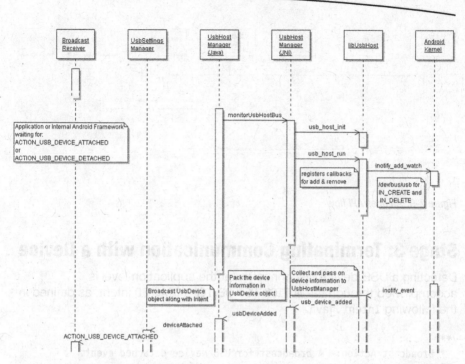

Figure 2-8. A USB_DEVICE_ATTACHED intent

When the Android system boots up, the UsbService framework creates a
UsbHostManager instance, and subsequently the onLoad function registers
UsbHostManager callbacks using register_android_server_UsbHostManager.
The registered callback will be called when a device is detected, along with
the device information. This information is used by the UsbHostManager to
generate the device-attached intent.

Now that you understand how the Android USB host framework detects
a USB device connection, you're ready to learn how to open and
communicate with a connected device.

Stage 2: Communicating with a Device

After a USB device connection is detected, the next stage is to
communicate with the device. Inside the UsbHostManager framework, all
communications are routed via the libusbhost library. The libusbhost library
interacts with the device using the device's file system of the Android kernel.
Figure 2-9 describes the control flow when a device open API is invoked.

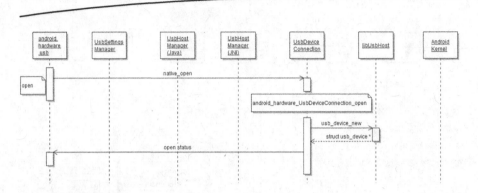

Figure 2-9. An open API flow

Stage 3: Terminating Communication with a Device

Detecting a USB device disconnection at the application level is accomplished through the ACTION_USB_DEVICE_DETACHED intent, as defined in the following Intent.java.

```
/**
 * Broadcast Action:  A broadcast for USB device detached event.
 *
 * This intent is sent when a USB device is detached from the USB
 * bus when in host mode.
 * <ul>
 * <li> {@link #EXTRA_DEVICE} containing the {@link android.hardware.usb.
UsbDevice}
 * for the detached device
 * </ul>
 */
public static final String ACTION_USB_DEVICE_DETACHED =
        "android.hardware.usb.action.USB_DEVICE_DETACHED";
```

Disconnection of a USB device is detected at the kernel level, and the kernel removes the device file entry from the /dev/bus/usb folder. The inotify system detects the change in the file system and notifies the libusbhost library monitor function. The callback function (usb_device_removed), which is registered for device removal by the UsbHostManager framework, tells the UsbHostManager framework to generate the ACTION_USB_DEVICE_DETACHED intent using the UsbSettingsManager framework. Figure 2-10 illustrates how ACTION_USB_DEVICE_DETACHED is generated in the Android USB framework.

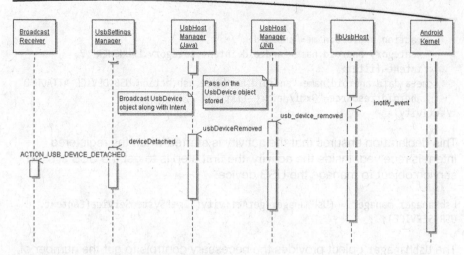

Figure 2-10. A USB_DEVICE_ATTACHED intent

Now that you've seen the complete flow of the USB host framework, you'll use what you've learned in a real application in the following section.

Sample 1: USBView

The purpose of this example is to demonstrate how an application can use the USB host APIs to interact with a USB device connected to the Android device. This application demonstrates how to implement a tool similar to the famous USBView tool available to the PC on Android. The functionality of the tool is to list the USB devices connected to the Android device along with the descriptor details.

Design and Flow

The first step in the process, as discussed earlier, is to detect the connection of a USB device in the system. This is achieved by registering for the ACTION_USB_DEVICE_ATTACHED intent and by declaring an intent filter in the AndroidManifest.xml file of the project, as shown here.

```
<activity
    android:name="com.example.usbview.ItemListActivity"
    android:label="@string/app_name" >
    <intent-filter>
      <action android:name="android.intent.action.MAIN" />
      <action android:name="android.hardware.usb.action.USB_DEVICE_ATTACHED" />
```

```
        <action android:name="android.h"/>
        <category android:name="android.intent.category.LAUNCHER" />
    </intent-filter>
    <meta-data android:name="android.hardware.usb.action.USB_DEVICE_ATTACHED"
        android:resource="@xml/device_list" />
</activity>
```

This declaration ensures that the activity is started when the registered intent is received. Inside the activity, the first step is to get the USB system service object to manage the USB device.

```
UsbManager manager = (UsbManager)getActivity().getSystemService(Context.
USB_SERVICE);
```

The UsbManager object provides the necessary controls to get the number of devices connected to Android system and then open the device.

```
Iterator<UsbDevice> deviceIterator = deviceList.values().iterator();
boolean test = deviceIterator.hasNext();
DummyContent.clearItem();
if (test) {
    while(deviceIterator.hasNext()) {
        int i = 0, ret=10;
        UsbDevice device = deviceIterator.next();
        UsbDeviceConnection connection = manager.openDevice(device);
```

Once the connection is established with the device, you can send control messages to retrieve the descriptors.

```
try {
 ret = connection.controlTransfer(0x80, 0x06, 1, 0,buffer, 18, 50000);
 Toast.makeText(getActivity().getBaseContext(),""+ret,2).show();
}
```

The descriptor received is then displayed in the list, as shown in Figure 2-11.

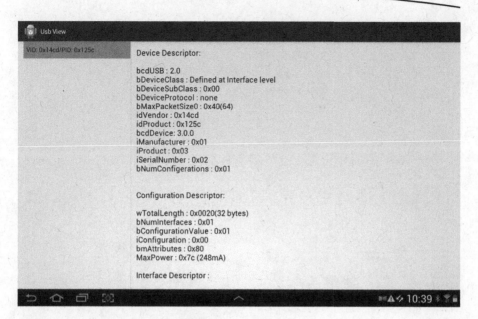

Figure 2-11. USBView Application snapshot

The complete code and project are available at http://www.apress.com/
9781430262084 and at https://git.techfugen.com/cgit/Android/apps/git/
usbview.git/. You can download the code and then send patches and add
functionality to the project.

Conclusion

The USB service framework implements leaf-level functionalities required for
the Android USB framework and forms the base framework that is used by
other frameworks. In this chapter, the USB device manager section explored
how different USB functions are managed. Later chapters discuss USB
Android accessory, USB storage, and USB tethering and will elaborate on
this device framework.

The host manager framework performs the simple work of detecting
insertion and removal of USB devices to the Android system. As discussed
in the USB host manager section and demonstrated through the example,
the host framework exposes the USB device connected to the application
framework. Chapter 3, "USB Storage" further explores the MTP host mode,
which will help further extend your understanding of USB host mode.

The USB Service framework also contains methods that implement permissions
and filters for the USB and accessory devices connected to the system. You
can read about how these filters are employed by the Android USB framework
in the UsbSettingsManager implementation in the following file: frameworks/
base/services/java/com/android/server/usb/UsbSettingsManager.java.

## Chapter 3

USB Storage

What You Will Learn:

- USB Storage Overview
- USB Mass Storage
  - a. USB Mass Storage Overview
  - b. USB Mass Storage Device Android Framework
  - c. USB Mass Storage Host Android Framework
- USB Media Transfer Protocol (MTP)
  - a. USB MTP Overview
  - b. USB MTP Device Android Framework
  - c. USB MTP Host Android Framework
- Example 1: Switch to UMS and MTP Mode
- Example 2: MTP Host Application

Young or old, most mobile users use their mobile devices as music players, cameras, and even for watching videos. To support these user scenarios, a device has to provide ample storage space and the provision to access and manage those storage spaces. Most mobile devices support two types of shared storage spaces, namely internal fixed memory and external shared memory, through standard SD card slots. Applications like cameras, music players, and video players use these storage spaces to store and retrieve data. Mobile devices provide transport mechanisms like USB and Bluetooth for end users to transfer data between the mobile device and a host PC.

In an Android-powered device, according to Android's CDD (Compatibility Definition Document, which is discussed in Chapter 1), an Android-powered device should provide a way to access the contents of shared storage from a host computer using USB protocols, such as USB Mass Storage (UMS) or Media Transfer Protocol (MTP). If the device does not support a USB port, it can support media sharing to the host PC using other means, such as via a network file system.

As detailed in Chapter 1, an Android-powered device can act in two USB modes, namely as a USB device or as a USB host. When a user connects an Android-powered device to a PC host, the Android device is in USB device mode. In USB device mode, the Android device shares the storage either through MTP or UMS mode. From Android version 4.0 (Ice Cream Sandwich), the Android CDD mandated MTP as the default method to share the storage space over USB as shown in the snippet below. Sometimes OEMs provide an option for switching from MTP to UMS and vice versa, which allows users to choose any protocol.

=============Android CDD Snippet=============

7.6.2. Application Shared Storage

Regardless of the form of shared storage that is used, device implementations must provide some mechanism to access the contents of shared storage from a host computer, such as USB Mass Storage (UMS) or Media Transfer Protocol (MTP). Device implementations may use USB mass storage, but should still use Media Transfer Protocol.

=============Android CDD Snippet=============

When a USB flash drive or an MTP Android-powered device (say another mobile device) is connected to an Android-powered device, the Android-powered device is in USB host mode. In this scenario, the Android-powered device has to provide a nominal 5V on the USB port's VBUS line. Note that in USB device mode, the host PC will provide power to the Android-powered device. Figure 3-1 illustrates these two different modes.

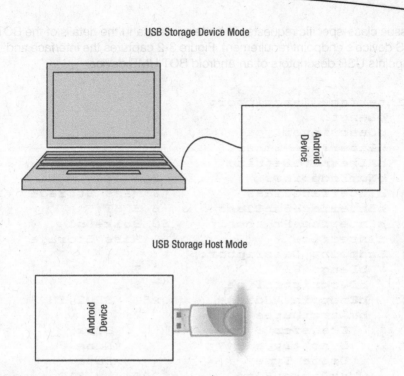

USB Storage Device Mode

USB Storage Host Mode

Figure 3-1. Two different USB storage setups

This chapter explores how these two USB protocols (UMS and MTP) are used to manage the shared storage space in both USB host and device modes. Unlike other chapters, since this chapter deals with multiple protocols, the UMS operation in both USB host and USB device mode followed by MTP mode is discussed.

USB Mass Storage (UMS) Overview

One of the most popular USB devices is the USB flash drive, which is a handy device that is used to store and transfer data from a host PC. The USB Mass Storage (UMS) class specification, defined by the USB-IF, provides an overview of how a mass storage device has to behave on an USB bus. Of the various protocols supported by the UMS class, devices like a USB flash drive or a mobile device support the Bulk-Only Transport (BOT) protocol defined in the USB-IF's mass storage class Bulk-Only Transport specification. The name comes from the fact that the protocol uses a bulk IN and a bulk OUT endpoint for all data transfer. Other, rarely used, UMS class protocols use interrupt transfers in addition to bulk transfers. The UMS protocol also uses the default control pipe to clear a STALL condition on the bulk endpoints and to issue class-specific requests. To better understand the details of the BOT UMS device's endpoint requirement, Figure 3-2 captures the interface and endpoints USB descriptors of an Android BOT UMS device.

```
Interface Descriptor:
   bLength                  9
   bDescriptorType          4
   bInterfaceNumber         0
   bAlternateSetting        0
   bNumEndpoints            2
   bInterfaceClass          8 Mass Storage
   bInterfaceSubClass       6 SCSI
   bInterfaceProtocol      80 Bulk-Only
   iInterface               1 Mass Storage
   Endpoint Descriptor:
      bLength                  7
      bDescriptorType          5
      bEndpointAddress      0x81  EP 1 IN
      bmAttributes             2
         Transfer Type            Bulk
         Synch Type               None
         Usage Type               Data
      wMaxPacketSize        0x0200  1x 512 bytes
      bInterval                0
   Endpoint Descriptor:
      bLength                  7
      bDescriptorType          5
      bEndpointAddress      0x01  EP 1 OUT
      bmAttributes             2
         Transfer Type            Bulk
         Synch Type               None
         Usage Type               Data
      wMaxPacketSize        0x0200  1x 512 bytes
      bInterval                1
```

Figure 3-2. The interface and endpoint descriptors for an Android USB mass storage device

From the descriptors, you will notice the descriptor's bInterfaceSubClass field indicates that the device uses the SCSI protocol and the bInterfaceProtocol field indicates that the interface protocol is Bulk-Only Transport. The descriptor also shows that the device uses bulk endpoints with a maximum packet size (bMaxPacketSize) of 512. High-speed devices must set bMaxPacketSize to 512.

Now that you've read about the interface and endpoint details of a UMS BOT Android device, the next section explains the UMS BOT protocol. It is made up of two important components, the command block wrapper (CBW) and the command status wrapper (CSW).

Command Block Wrapper (CBW)

The command block wrapper (CBW) is 31 bytes of data that contain a command and its associated information. The CBW holds details like a fixed signature, length of data expected, direction of data transfer, the logical unit, and a payload that may contain a SCSI command to be executed. To better understand the CBW, take a look at Figure 3-3, which shows a snapshot from a USB protocol analyzer (Ellisys). It provides the finer details of the various fields of the CBW.

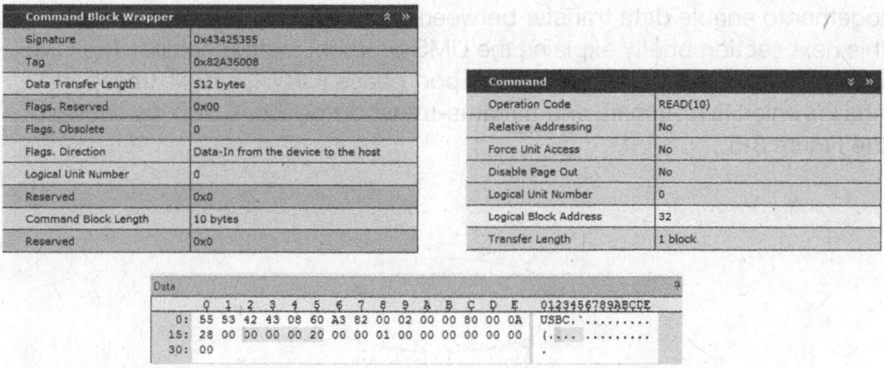

Command Block Wrapper	≈ »
Signature	0x43425355
Tag	0x82A36008
Data Transfer Length	512 bytes
Flags. Reserved	0x00
Flags. Obsolete	0
Flags. Direction	Data-In from the device to the host
Logical Unit Number	0
Reserved	0x0
Command Block Length	10 bytes
Reserved	0x0

Command	≈ »
Operation Code	READ(10)
Relative Addressing	No
Force Unit Access	No
Disable Page Out	No
Logical Unit Number	0
Logical Block Address	32
Transfer Length	1 block

```
Data                                                                   ≈
        0  1  2  3  4  5  6  7  8  9  A  B  C  D  E   0123456789ABCDE
    0:  55 53 42 43 08 60 A3 82 00 02 00 00 80 00 0A  USBC.`.........
   15:  28 00 00 00 00 20 00 00 01 00 00 00 00 00 00  (.... .........
   30:  00
```

Figure 3-3. The finer details of a CBW

Figure 3-3 provides a breakdown of a CBW captured using a USB bus analyzer. The example CBW shows a payload containing a SCSI READ command sent from the USB host requesting 512 bytes of data.

Command Status Wrapper (CSW)

The Command Status Wrapper (CSW) is a 13-byte response to the prior command received and can be preceded by a data phase. The command status block holds information like a fixed signature, information about the data transfer, along with the status of the command. So you can better understand the CSW, Figure 3-4 shows a snapshot from a USB protocol analyzer (Ellisys). It provides the finer details of the various fields of the CSW.

Status Block Wrapper	≪ ≫
Signature	0x53425355
Tag	0x82A36008
Data Residue	0 bytes
Status	Command Passed

Details | Search | Export | Summary

Data

```
     0  1  2  3  4  5  6  7  8  9  A  B  C  D    0123456789ABCD
0:  55 53 42 53 08 60 A3 82 00 00 00 00 00       USBS.`........
```

Figure 3-4. The finer details of a CSW

Now that you understand how the BOT protocol and the SCSI protocol work together to enable data transfer between a USB host and a UMS device, this next section briefly explains the UMS protocol state machine. The UMS BOT protocol uses a command-transport phase (CBW), a data-transport phase (which is optional), and a status-transport phase (CSW), as shown in the Figure 3-5.

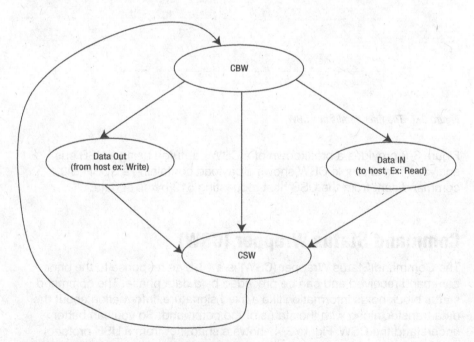

Figure 3-5. A state diagram of a UMS BOT protocol

The protocol starts with the USB host sending a CBW to the UMS class device. Based on the command received, the USB device or host may send data in the data-transport phase, or the data-transport phase may be absent. To complete the command, the device sends a CSW in the status-transport phase. All phases use bulk endpoints.

The following section explains how this protocol is implemented in an Android environment, in both USB host and device modes. The subsequent section explores the sequence of activities within the Android framework when in UMS mode, and later concludes with an example that shows how to switch an Android device between USB Mass Storage mode and Media Transfer Protocol (MTP) mode.

Android Mass Storage Framework

The Android Mass Storage framework essentially consists of two categories—the Android framework that manages the UMS protocol when the Android device is in USB device mode and the Android Mass Storage framework that manages the UMS protocol when the Android device is in USB host mode. In both cases, the UMS protocol is completely managed by the Android kernel layer and the Android framework is either used to enable the functionality or to present the storage to the user. The following section explores both the USB device and the USB host use cases in detail.

Android USB Mass Storage Device Framework

The Android USB Mass Storage device framework consists of both the Android and kernel frameworks, with most of the work done at the Linux kernel USB driver level. The Android USB framework in a USB device mass storage use case performs basic functional management and provides the necessary information to the user. The actual BOT protocol and interaction with the storage device (such as an MMC card) is taken care at the kernel level. Figure 3-6 provides an architectural view of the Android USB Mass Storage device framework.

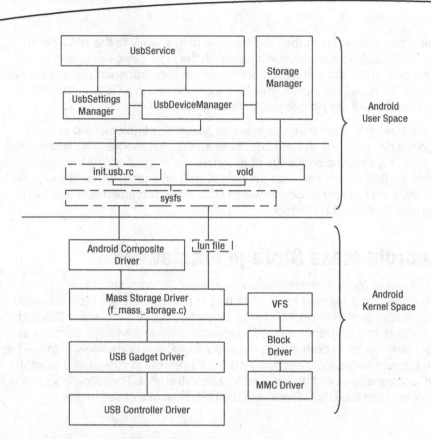

Figure 3-6. An Android USB Mass Storage device framework

The Android USB Mass Storage device framework implementation is not a separate file, but is interleaved within the UsbDeviceManager and the UsbService frameworks implemented in the following files: frameworks/base/services/java/com/android/server/usb/UsbDeviceManager.java and frameworks/base/services/java/com/android/server/usb/UsbService.java.

The complete UMS class implementation is done at the Android kernel level. The implementation is available in the drivers/usb/gadget/f_mass_storage.c file.

The kernel driver implementation provides options to manage the number of logical units (LUNs) to be supported by the driver and the sysfs interface to help associate a storage location for each LUN. The typical representation of a LUN is a drive letter. The following file is used to associate the storage block to the UMS driver: /sys/class/android_usb/android0/f_mass_storage/lun/file.

The storage part of the UMS BOT device implementation is managed by the MMC driver available in the /driver/mmc folder. This MMC driver creates entries for the storage volumes in /dev/block for each partition. The storage part of the UMS is managed by the StorageManager framework and by the volume daemon (system/vold) that's present in the frameworks/base/core/java/android/os/storage/StorageManager.java, frameworks/base/services/java/com/android/server/MountService.java, and system/vold/VolumeManager.cpp files.

The MountService registers itself for the USB intent called UsbManager.ACTION_USB_STATE, which is broadcasted to indicate changes in the USB framework. The MountService waits for the USB_CONNECTED state, as shown in the following snippet, and along with the storage manager, prepares the Android framework to be ready for sharing the memory space with the UMS gadget driver. The StorageManager class also uses an internal event called EVENT_UMS_CONNECTION_CHANGED to communicate UMS state changes. The volume daemon (vold) framework detects any addition of storage volume and helps associate the storage medium to the UMS kernel driver.

```
// Watch for USB changes on primary volume
final StorageVolume primary = getPrimaryPhysicalVolume();
if (primary != null && primary.allowMassStorage()) {
  mContext.registerReceiver(
     mUsbReceiver, new IntentFilter(UsbManager.ACTION_USB_STATE), null,
     mHandler);
}
```

The Android framework system UI, which presents users with the UMS feature in the notification bar and enables them to mount storage to a UMS driver, is available in the following file locations: frameworks/base/packages/SystemUI/src/com/android/systemui/usb/StorageNotification.java and /frameworks/base/packages/SystemUI/src/com/android/systemui/usb/UsbStorageActivity.java.

The system UI relies on the USB_STATE change intent broadcasted by the Android USB framework to dynamically update the UI to present the UMS feature.

The next section explores the sequence of internal activities that happen when an Android device acts as a USB mass storage device.

Sharing the Storage

Inside the Android framework, when the device boots or switches to UMS mode, the framework brings up the UMS functionality on the user interface. This is because an SD card is mounted inside the device and for the UMS to use the storage space, the storage has to be unshared and mounted to the UMS driver. Figure 3-7 illustrates how a storage location is associated with the UMS gadget driver in order to share memory over USB to a host PC using the UMS protocol.

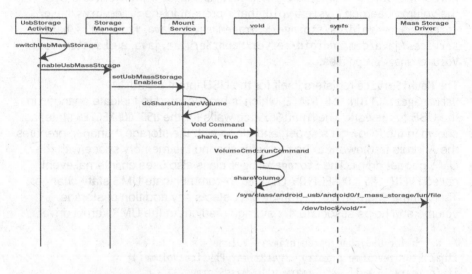

Figure 3-7. A sequence of activity to mount storage over UMS

Communication between the volume daemon (vold) and the Android Storage framework (MountService) is achieved by creating a connection to the daemon using NativeConnectionFramework, as shown here:

```
/*
* Create the connection to vold with a maximum queue of twice the
* amount of containers we'd ever expect to have. This keeps an
* "asec list" from blocking a thread repeatedly.
*/
mConnector = new NativeDaemonConnector(this, "vold", MAX_CONTAINERS * 2,
VOLD_TAG, 25);
```

The mounting of storage is initiated by the user through the UI framework, which passes the information to the StorageManager and subsequently to the MountService, as illustrated in Figure 3-7. The MountService framework forms a share command and passes to the daemon through the daemon connector. Inside the daemon (vold), the command is received and interpreted by system/vold/CommandListener.cpp and invokes shareVolume to associate the storage to the UMS gadget driver.

DID YOU KNOW?

When the volume daemon associates storage space to the UMS gadget driver using shareVolume, the function also disables caching by setting /proc/sys/vm/dirty_ratio to '0' The diff history (a28056b38275003895ff5d9576681aca01544822) shows that this has been changed to improve UI performance. This means that UMS will perform slower, compared to previous versions of Android. Linux provides a default dirty_ratio value of '20' To get better UMS performance, you can restore the default value.

Android USB Mass Storage Host Framework

Android framework officially provided its USB host requirement from the Android ICS version by providing host APIs. But this doesn't restrict the use of the Android USB Mass Storage host mode, as long as the device hardware includes a USB host controller and the necessary drivers are enabled within the Android kernel. In the case of the Android UMS host mode, all the necessary implementation is available inside the Android Linux kernel and the UMS device shows up on the Android framework as a disk device. Figure 3-8 illustrates various blocks of USB mass storage.

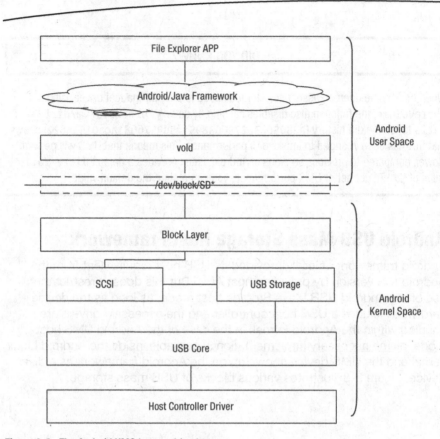

Figure 3-8. The Android UMS host architechture

When a UMS device—say a USB flash drive—is connected to an Android-powered device, the UMS device gets enumerated and the usb-storage USB storage driver module associates with the device. The USB storage subsequently registers to the SCSI driver and presents the USB device as a block device to the user space using the block layer. Thus, a complete USB abstraction takes place within the kernel layer and the device is presented as a block device to the user framework. No special Android USB framework is required for managing or viewing a UMS device in an Android-powered device.

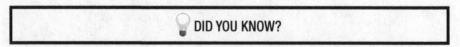

DID YOU KNOW?

Whenever your Android-powered device claims it is OTG (On The Go) (host mode support) and cannot enumerate a USB flash drive connected to it due to power issues, add a "self-powered" hub between the Android-powered device and your USB flash drive. This trick should help the Android-powered device enumerate the USB flash device.

USB Media Transfer Protocol (MTP) Overview

Media Transfer Protocol, or MTP, was developed by Microsoft to transfer media files along with its meta-data using a client/server model. MTP was initially developed as an extension of Picture Transfer Protocol (PTP) and was later adapted as a USB class by the USB implementer forum. When an Android device uses UMS implementation to share storage, it shares the storage completely with full control to the PC host, which gets exclusive rights to delete or format. This can lead to accidental loss of data or create a situation in which users can't access the memory when connected as a UMS device. However, MTP provides a method to share storage in a more secure and structured way. This means that during MTP operation, the storage space is completely managed by the Android-powered device, unlike with the UMS implementation.

MTP adopts an "operation-data-response" model for its communication, where the USB host MTP implementation is referred to as the initiator and the USB device MTP implementation is referred as the responder. A detailed explanation of the communication model is provided in the subsequent section. Figure 3-9 illustrates the two MTP roles that an Android-powered device can play.

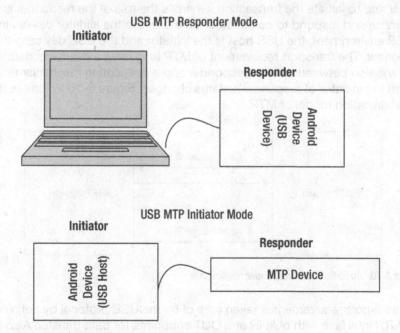

USB MTP Responder Mode

Initiator

Responder

Android Device (USB Device)

USB MTP Initiator Mode

Initiator

Responder

Android Device (USB Host)

MTP Device

Figure 3-9. An Android powered device's different MTP roles

After having briefly introduced MTP, this chapter provides the details of the MTP specification, and then explores the internals of the Android MTP framework. At the end of the chapter, an application that demonstrates the MTP initiator APIs, provided by the Android framework to communicate to an MTP device, is explored.

Media Transfer Protocol Specification Overview

MTP was developed with the intention of providing seemly communication that allows for the sharing of storage contents targeting devices like portable media players, mobile phones, and so on. It is also important to note that the MTP specification was defined as a transport-agnostic protocol, which means the protocol can operate on a USB, a network interface, and similar. The Media Transfer Protocol specification provided by the USB-IF defines the implementation of MTP over USB and is available in http://www.usb.org/developers/docs/devclass_docs/MTPv1_1.zip. Thus, this MTP specification defines how MTP works over USB.

The communication model of MTP is peer-to-peer, and in that communication setup, one device is referred to as the initiator and the other device is referred to as the responder. The role of the initiator is to act as a server and to initiate the transaction, whereas the role of the responder is to service and respond to commands like a client to the initiator device. In a USB environment, the USB host is the initiator and the USB device is the responder. The transport requirement of MTP is to have a seamless data transmission between initiator/responder and a notification mechanism to inform the initiator of responder's status changes. Figure 3-10 illustrates the communication model of MTP.

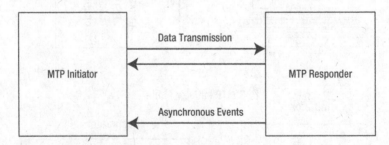

Figure 3-10. An initiator and responder relationship

The transport requirement is taken care of by the USB protocol by defining the MTP interface with bulk IN and OUT endpoints for data transfer. Also defined is an interrupt endpoint for asynchronous notification of the status information. Figure 3-11 shows an MTP interface descriptor and subordinate endpoint descriptors for an Android device.

```
Interface Descriptor:
   bLength              9
   bDescriptorType      4
   bInterfaceNumber     0
   bAlternateSetting    0
   bNumEndpoints        3
   bInterfaceClass      255 Vendor Specific Class
   bInterfaceSubClass   255 Vendor Specific Subclass
   bInterfaceProtocol   0
   iInterface           5 MTP
 Endpoint Descriptor:
   bLength              7
   bDescriptorType      5
   bEndpointAddress     0x81 EP 1 IN
   bmAttributes         2
    Transfer Type         Bulk
    Synch Type            None
    Usage Type            Data
   wMaxPacketSize       0x0200 1x 512 bytes
   bInterval            0
 Endpoint Descriptor:
   bLength              7
   bDescriptorType      5
   bEndpointAddress     0x01 EP 1 OUT
   bmAttributes         2
    Transfer Type         Bulk
    Synch Type            None
    Usage Type            Data
   wMaxPacketSize       0x0200 1x 512 bytes
   bInterval            1

 Endpoint Descriptor:
   bLength              7
   bDescriptorType      5
   bEndpointAddress     0x83 EP 3 IN
   bmAttributes         3
    Transfer Type         Interrupt
    Synch Type            None
    Usage Type            Data
   wMaxPacketSize       0x001c 1x 28 bytes
   bInterval            6
```

Figure 3-11. An interface descriptor and endpoint descriptors for an Android MTP device

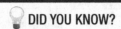

DID YOU KNOW?

Though the USB-IF MTP specification (section 2.7) states that no specific or proprietary USB string descriptor is required for USB enumeration, a MTP USB device has to provide a string descriptor with a signature string to enumerate successfully with a Microsoft Windows PC. (See http://androidxref.com/kernel_3.4/xref/drivers/usb/gadget/f_mtp.c#220.)

Now that you've read a brief overview of an MTP setup, it's time to learn about MTP and its operation. As an abstract over an underlying transport, MTP is also independent of a file system and the file type of the media, and the file is treated as a binary object. An MTP binary object also holds additional meta-information about the file, thus enabling the protocol to act on the binary object without understanding the format of the binary file. A combination of the binary file and its meta-data is referred to as an MTP object. To manage and gain access to MTP objects, MTP defines a set of command and response protocols.

To have an understanding of MTP, consider a basic scenario of how an object is pulled from a responder to an initiator, and go through the command/response process. Figure 3-12 illustrates the exchanges happening when an object is retried from a responder device.

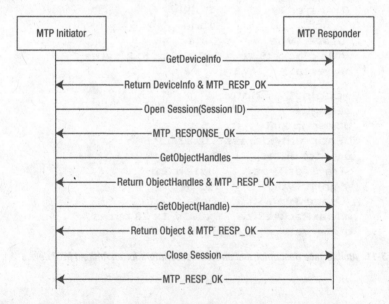

Figure 3-12. The sequence of activities for retrieving an object from a responder

After successful enumeration of a responder, the first command sent by the initiator is to get the device (responder) information using the GetDeviceInfo command. Upon receiving it, the responder collects its information and sends it back to the initiator in a format defined by MTP specification. The data is also followed by a notification on the status of the command execution, MTP_RESP_OK, upon successful completion. Subsequently, to begin any operation, the initiator has to start a session with an OpenSession command. Once a session is established, the initiator collects handles of all the objects and retrieves interested objects from the responder using the GetObject command.

The command and response sequence is carried out in three transaction phases: i) the Operation request phase, ii) the Data phase, and iii) the Response phase. The Data phase is optional and is valid only for certain commands occurring between the Request and the Response phases.

The next section explores how this protocol is implemented within the Android framework.

Android MTP Responder Framework

According to the Android CDD, an Android device should implement MTP to share media with a host PC. When an Android device implements MTP, it should be compatible with the Android reference MTP host implementation. Inside the Android USB framework, the MTP responder framework implementation is available in the following folders:

```
frameworks/base/media/java/android/mtp/
frameworks/av/media/mtp/
frameworks/base/media/jni/
```

The key file in the Android USB MTP Responder framework that manages responder activity is MTPServer, and the kernel implementation of the MTP is available in drivers/usb/gadget/f_mtp.c. Like other USB functionalities, USB state management and the enabling of USB functionality is interleaved with the UsbService and UsbDeviceManager implementations. Communication between the kernel MTP module and the Android MTP responder framework is through the device file called mtp_usb, which implements the file operation to perform data operations.

Figure 3-13 illustrates the various modules of the MTP responder framework, along with the USB kernel modules. The subsequent section explains the different class frameworks involved in implementing an MTP responder.

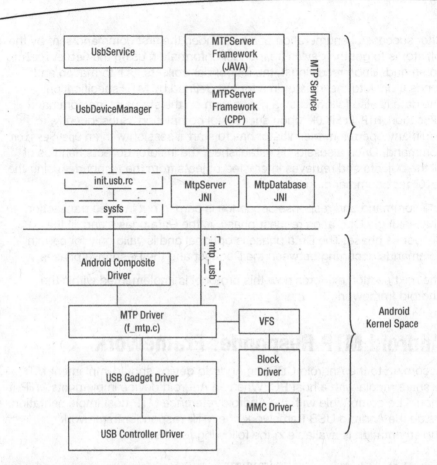

Figure 3-13. The Android MTP Responder framework

MTPServer

The MTPServer class is the core framework in the responder implementation. It consists of the following files:

```
frameworks/base/media/java/android/mtp/MtpServer.java
frameworks/av/media/mtp/MtpServer.cpp
frameworks/base/media/jni/android_mtp_MtpServer.cpp
```

The MTPServer's JNI implementation, acts as the interface to connect with the kernel driver. The database is invoked when the MTPServer class gets instantiated. The MTPServer CPP implementation manages the complete command response interaction with the initiator.

MTPRequestPacket

The `MTPRequestPacket` class is implemented for handling the request phase of the MTP transaction for both the responder and the initiator, and the implementation is conditionally compiled using macros. The implementation can be found in the `frameworks/av/media/mtp/MtpRequestPacket.cpp` file.

MTPResponsePacket

The `MTPResponsePacket` class is implemented for the response phase of the MTP transaction for both the responder and the initiator. The implementation for both responder and initiator is conditionally compiled using macros. The implementation can be found in the `frameworks/av/media/mtp/MtpResponsePacket.cpp` file.

MTPDataPacket

The `MTPDataPacket` class is implemented for handling the data phase of the MTP transaction for both the responder and the initiator. The implementation for both responder and initiator is conditionally compiled using macros. The implementation can be found in the `frameworks/av/media/mtp/MtpDataPacket.cpp` file.

MTPDatabase

The `MTPDatabase` class is implemented to handle binary objects and the meta-data stored in the storage of the Android device. The implementation can be found in the `frameworks/base/media/java/android/mtp/MtpDatabase.java` and `frameworks/base/media/jni/android_mtp_MtpDatabase.cpp` files.

MTPEventPacket

The `MTPEventPacket` class is implemented for handling asynchronous events for both the responder and the initiator. The implementation for both responder and initiator is conditionally compiled using macros. The implementation can be found in the `frameworks/av/media/mtp/MtpEventPacket.cpp` file.

Now that you have an understanding of the various blocks of the Android USB MTP responder framework, the following section explores how these modules communicate with each other during an MTP transaction.

MTP Responder: Command/Response Sequence

The Android USB MTP device framework implementation is completely managed through the MTPServer class, which includes transaction management, managing the storage, and so on. The responder framework is started by MTPService whenever the Android USB framework enables MTP functionality. This functionality is managed by MtpReceiver.java and MTPService.java, available in packages/providers/MediaProvider/src/com/android/providers/media/.

Once the MTPService associates the database with the MTPServer and instantiates the MTPServer, the Android device is ready to serve MTP initiator commands. After a successful start, the MTPServer waits in an infinite loop in the run member function for MTP command request from the initiator. To understand this framework, we'll consider a simple command called GetDeviceInfo and explore the sequence of activity within the MTP responder framework.

Figure 3-14 illustrates the complete sequence of activity within the Android USB MTP responder framework when a GetDeviceInfo command is received.

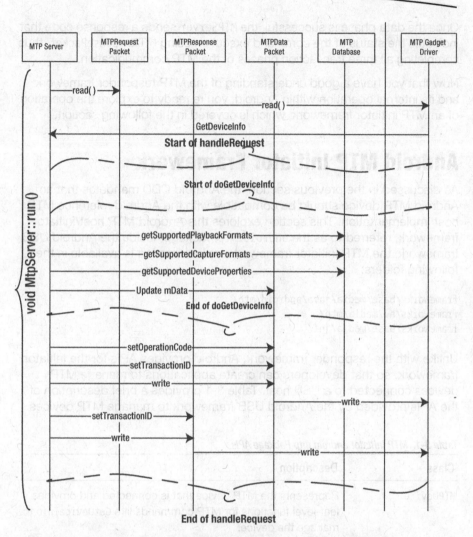

Figure 3-14. A sequence of activities in the Android USB MTP responder framework

Once the command is received by MTPServer, based on the command, an optional data phase is managed. The command is parsed using the handleRequest function.

In case of GetDeviceInfo, the command is managed by the doGetDeviceInfo function, which collects information necessary for the response. The function uses MTPDatabase to collect information like playback format and device properties, and updates the MTPDataPacket to send it over to the Android USB gadget driver.

Once the data phase is successful, the MTPServer sends a response code that indicates the status of the command execution using MTPResponsePacket, thus completing all three transaction phases of the MTP communication.

Now that you have a good understanding of the MTP responder framework and its internal operation within Android, you're ready to explore the operation of an MTP initiator framework, which is covered in the following section.

Android MTP Initiator Framework

As discussed in the previous section, the Android CDD mandates that an Android MTP device should be compatible with the Android reference MTP host implementation. This section explores this Android MTP host/initiator framework, referred to as the android.mtp package. Inside the Android USB framework, the MTP initiator framework implementation is available in the following folders:

```
frameworks/base/media/java/android/mtp/
frameworks/av/media/mtp/
frameworks/base/media/jni/
```

Unlike with the responder framework, Android provides APIs for the Initiator framework, so that developers can create applications to manage MTP devices connected to a USB host. Table 3-1 provides a brief description of the APIs provided by the Android USB framework to manage MTP devices.

Table 3-1. MTP Initiator android.mtp Package APIs

Class	Description
MTPDevice	Represents the MTP device that is connected and provides leaf-level functions for MTP commands like GetDeviceInfo to manage the device.
MTPStorageInfo	Retrieves details related to the storage medium that the MTP device is exporting, with leaf functions like getStorageID, getFreeSpace, and so on.
MTPDeviceInfo	Holds information about the MTP device information, as defined in section 5.2.2 of the MTP specification.
MTPObjectInfo	Holds information about the MTP object information, as defined in section 5.3.1 of the MTP specification.

Like the Android USB MTP device framework, the MTP host framework and MTP class functionality are completely implemented at the Android framework level, and transport over USB is done over the Android kernel's usb-core module. Figure 3-15 illustrates the MTP initiator architecture within the Android framework.

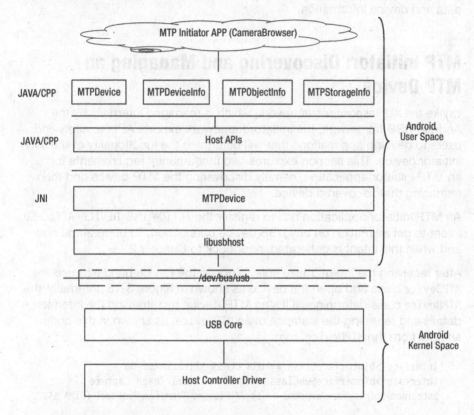

Figure 3-15. The Android USB MTP initiator architechture

As illustrated in Figure 3-15, the kernel layer shares the MTP device connected to the Android framework over the /dev/bus/usb files, which is further accessed by the initiator framework using the libusbhost library. To understand in more detail how a USB device is discovered by the Android USB framework, refer back to Chapter 2, "Discovering and Managing USB Within Android."

It is also important to understand that unlike the responder framework, where an MTPService framework binds itself when the Android device framework enables MTP function, an MTP initiator is the bare framework provided for an application developer to develop applications using the APIs exported by the framework. Thus, for an Android USB MTP initiator architecture to be complete, an application has to be installed that can discover an MTP device and retrieve device and object information from the device.

The following section explores how the sequence of events occur in an MTP initiator application from discovering and managing the device by retrieving data and device information.

MTP Initiator: Discovering and Managing an MTP Device

Unlike the MTPResponder framework, which is managed internally by the Android USB framework, the initiator framework exports APIs to allow end users to develop applications that will determine the functionality of the MTP initiator device. This section explores two fundamental requirements for an MTP initiator application, namely discovering the MTP device and then managing the discovered device.

An MTP initiator application has to register the ACTION_USB_DEVICE_ATTACHED intent to get intimation on any USB device connection. To understand how and when this intent is generated, refer back to Chapter 2.

After receiving the intent, make sure to obtain the device handle to use the MTPDevice class and open the device as shown in Figure 3-16. Internally, the MTPDevice class determines if it's an MTP device by retrieving the interface details and returning the instance of an MTPDevice, as shown in this code snippet from the MTPDevice.cpp:

```
if (interface->bInterfaceClass == USB_CLASS_STILL_IMAGE &&
    interface->bInterfaceSubClass == 1 && // Still Image Capture
    interface->bInterfaceProtocol == 1) // Picture Transfer Protocol (PIMA 15470)
{
    char* manufacturerName = usb_device_get_manufacturer_name(device);
    char* productName = usb_device_get_product_name(device);
    ALOGD("Found camera: \"%s\" \"%s\"\n", manufacturerName, productName);
    free(manufacturerName);
    free(productName);
} else if (interface->bInterfaceClass == 0xFF &&
    interface->bInterfaceSubClass == 0xFF &&
    interface->bInterfaceProtocol == 0) {
```

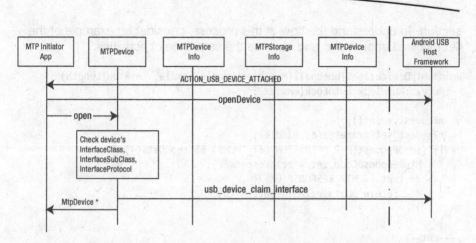

Figure 3-16. *The sequence of activities when an intiator application opens an MTP device*

After ensuring that the interface is an MTP, the MTPDevice class claims the interface and returns to an MTPDevice object.

After claiming the interface, the next step is to manage the MTP device. Figure 3-17 illustrates the sequence of activities within the Android MTP Initiator framework that make up a complete transaction.

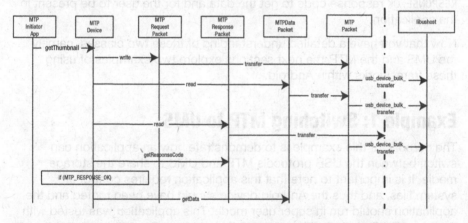

Figure 3-17. *A command/response sequence within an Android MTP initiator framework*

A command transaction involves multiple classes, namely MTPRequestPacket, MTPResponsePacket, and MTPDataPacket. These classes implement the three stages of MTP transactions as described in the beginning of the MTP section. To understand the flow of this process, consider an example of the GetThumbnail command and observe the sequence of activities.

```
void* MtpDevice::getThumbnail(MtpObjectHandle handle, int& outLength) {
    Mutex::Autolock autoLock(mMutex);

    mRequest.reset();
    mRequest.setParameter(1, handle);
    if (sendRequest(MTP_OPERATION_GET_THUMB) && readData()) {
        MtpResponseCode ret = readResponse();
        if (ret == MTP_RESPONSE_OK) {
            return mData.getData(outLength);
        }
    }
}
----cut----
```

When a command is received by the MTPDevice, it forms the request packet and invokes the write function of the MTPRequestPacket class. Internally, all of these packet classes are derived from an MTPPacket class, which acts as an interface for the low-level function, that is, the interface for libusbhost.

The next stage is to handle the data phase of the transaction. The readData function collects the data using an MTPDataPacket object. While these two phases are successfully completing, the MTPDevice waits for the MTP_RESPONSE_OK response code to get the data and for the user to be present in the application.

Now that you have a detailed understanding of these two classes, namely the UMS and the MTP, the next sections explore two examples of using these frameworks within Android.

Example 1: Switching MTP to UMS

The purpose of this example is to demonstrate how an application can switch between the USB protocols MTP and UMS to share the storage media. It is important to note that this application requires control of system files, and thus the Android device should have been rooted and the application should run in super user mode. This application was tested with Samsung Tab2, rooted with a custom Android from Cynogenmod, but this procedure should work with all devices.

Design and Flow

In a normal setup, if UMS is supported by an Android device's `init.usb.rc`, it will contain the following entries to manage USB functionality:

```
on property:sys.usb.config=mass_storage
    write /sys/class/android_usb/android0/enable 0
    write /sys/class/android_usb/android0/functions ${sys.usb.config}
    write /sys/class/android_usb/android0/enable 1
    setprop sys.usb.state ${sys.usb.config}

on property:sys.usb.config=mass_storage,adb
    write /sys/class/android_usb/android0/enable 0
    write /sys/class/android_usb/android0/functions ${sys.usb.config}
    write /sys/class/android_usb/android0/enable 1
    start adbd
    setprop sys.usb.state ${sys.usb.config}
```

This information at boot time is loaded within the Android framework and will be executed when the UMS (`mass_storage`) functionality is enabled by the Android framework or by a user. Most vendors do not provide support for UMS, and hence remove these type of entries from the `init*.rc` file.

Since the Android framework does not provide an option to set a particular USB function through interface functions for the application, direct sets have required functions using a super user library, thereby switching between required functions.

To Switch to UMS Mode

The following code ensures the switching of USB functionality to UMS mode:

```
OnClickListener mtp2ums = new OnClickListener() {

public void onClick(View arg0) {

    Toast.makeText(getBaseContext(),"MTP MSC Click",Toast.LENGTH_LONG).show();

    execCommandAsSU("echo 0 > /sys/class/android_usb/android0/enable");
    execCommandAsSU("echo mass_storage,adb > /sys/class/android_usb/android0/
    functions");
    execCommandAsSU("echo /dev/block/mmcblk1 > /sys/class/android_usb/
    android0/f_mass_storage/lun/file");
    execCommandAsSU("echo 1 > /sys/class/android_usb/android0/enable");
    execCommandAsSU("setprop sys.usb.state mass_storage,adb");

    };
};
```

For UMS functionality to work, the Android kernel looks for the storage to be shared with the host PC. This information is provided through a file that the kernel exports, called f_mass_storage/lun/file. The application associates the external SD card generally named mmcblk1p1 as follows:

```
execCommandAsSU("echo /dev/block/mmcblk1 > /sys/class/android_usb/
android0/f_mass_storage/lun/file");
```

This can be any valid block device that a user requires and can be identified by busy box tools.

To Switch to MTP Mode

The following code ensures switching back from USB functionality to MTP mode:

```
OnClickListener ums2mtp= new OnClickListener() {

public void onClick(View arg0) {
    Toast.makeText(getBaseContext(),"MSC MTP Click",Toast.LENGTH_LONG).show();
    execCommandAsSU("echo 0 > /sys/class/android_usb/android0/enable");
    execCommandAsSU("echo mtp,adb > /sys/class/android_usb/android0/functions");
    execCommandAsSU("echo 1 > /sys/class/android_usb/android0/enable");
    execCommandAsSU("setprop sys.usb.state mtp,adb");

    };
};
```

The complete code and project are available as part of the source code download available at http://www.apress.com/9781430262084 and on https://git.techfugen.com/cgit/Android/apps/git/mtp2ums.git/. You can download the code and send patches to add functionalities, like choosing appropriate storage, and so on, to the project. Figure 3-18 provides a snapshot of the application.

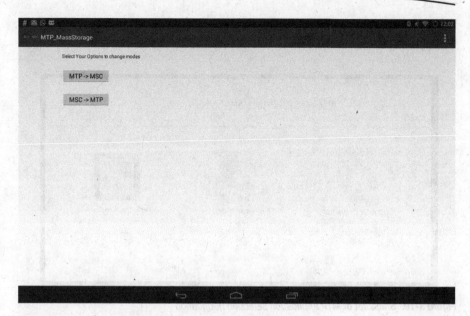

Figure 3-18. Snapshot of the MTP-MSC switch application

Example 2: MTP Initiator Application

The purpose of this example is to demonstrate how an application can use the android.mtp APIs to retrieve information from an MTP device's storage media. This "CameraBrowser" application is part of the Android framework and is available in frameworks/base/media/tests/CameraBrowser/src/com/android/camerabrowser/. As the detailed flow has been analyzed in the previous sections, this example presents only the key points along with the screen shots of the application in action.

Design and Flow

In this application, the Android device acts as a USB host. Therefore, the first step is to have broadcast listener to get notified for USB_DEVICE_ATTACHED intent that gets generated when a USB device is connected to an Android USB host. To receive notification for the intent the setup is done in the manifest, as in the file shown here:

```
</intent-filter>
  <intent-filter>
      <action android:name="android.hardware.usb.action.USB_DEVICE_ATTACHED" />
  </intent-filter>
  <meta-data android:name="android.hardware.usb.action.USB_DEVICE_ATTACHED"
      android:resource="@xml/device_filter" />
</activity>
```

When an MTP device is connected to an Android device that's running this application, the application gets notified, as shown in Figure 3-19.

Figure 3-19. Snapshot of MTP application selection notification

Once you choose the application that will communicate with the device, the application opens the device and adds the following to the user interface:

```
if (UsbManager.ACTION_USB_DEVICE_ATTACHED.equals(action)) {
    if (mtpDevice == null) {
      mtpDevice = openDeviceLocked(usbDevice);
    }
    if (mtpDevice != null) {
      for (Listener listener : mListeners) {
        listener.deviceAdded(mtpDevice);
      }
    }
}
```

The application then lists the connected device's detail retrieved as shown in Figure 3-20 using GetDeviceInfo in the text view, as shown here:

```
TextView textView2 = (TextView)view.findViewById(android.R.id.text2);
MtpDevice device = mDeviceList.get(position);
MtpDeviceInfo info = device.getDeviceInfo();
if (info != null) {
      textView1.setText(info.getManufacturer());
      textView2.setText(info.getModel());
} else {
```

Figure 3-20. A snapshot of the CameraBrowser application

Clicking on the device listed by the CameraBrowser application as in the above Figure 3-20 retrieves the media contents of the device using StorageBrowser class.

```
protected void onListItemClick(ListView l, View v, int position, long id) {
    Intent intent = new Intent(this, StorageBrowser.class);
    intent.putExtra("device", mDeviceList.get(position).getDeviceName());
    startActivity(intent);
}
```

StorageBrowser and ObjectBrowser scan through the media of the connected devices and present the information depicted in Figure 3-21.

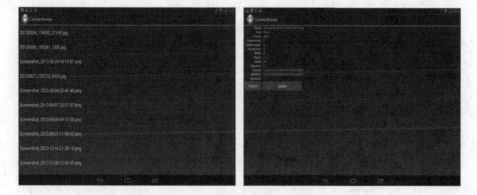

Figure 3-21. Snapshot of the CameraBroswer Storage window

Conclusion

This chapter provided detailed information on various USB storage operations and their framework along with the USB-IF defined class specification. As a developer you can now explore further on each USB classes and build your own application like a Media Player over USB or a application that allows to update details of the media files using MTP.

On the UMS class though Android has moved away from UMS device mode, it still keeps the framework intact so that a vendor could provide both functionalities for the user.

## Chapter 4

USB Tethering

What you will learn:

- USB tethering overview
- RNDIS specification overview
- Android USB tethering framework
- Example: Reverse tethering

Communication between any mobile device and a PC (Personal Computer) has always been a basic requirement for end users. Mobile devices use this communication generally to get a software update, to back up the data from a device, or even to charge the battery. On the other hand, a PC uses important data-communication features of a mobile device to gain access to the Internet. With the evolution of modem and wireless telephony technology (2G to 3G to 4G), mobile data communication devices have increased tremendously. With the Internet becoming part and parcel of everyone's life, mobile devices can provide seamless data connections with the aforementioned technologies. Thus, the process of sharing an Internet connection with a PC is referred as "tethering" in the mobile world. Mobile devices generally use tethers using USB (Universal Serial Bus), Wife, or Bluetooth as the transport medium in order to share the Internet. This chapter restricts itself to USB tethering.

When an Android mobile device tethers using USB, it enumerates as a Remote Network Driver Interface Specification (RNDIS) device. RNDIS is a Microsoft proprietary protocol for managing network communications. Figure 4-1 shows the menu option used to enable USB tethering on an Android device via the Wireless and networks option.

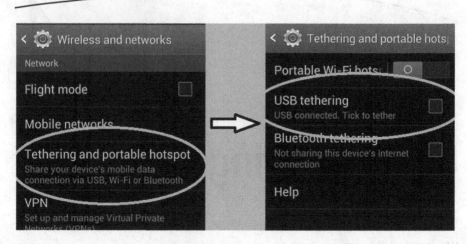

Figure 4-1. An option to enable Android USB tethering

After successful enumeration on a Windows PC, you can explore the control panel lists for the Android device as an RNDIS device. Figure 4-2 illustrates how a Windows Control Panel entry looks when a Samsung Android device is USB tethered to a machine using Windows.

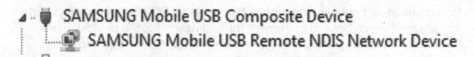

Figure 4-2. Windows OS Control Panel entry of a USB tethered device

---

💡 **DO YOU KNOW?**

The tethering driver installation is automatic in the case of Windows 7 or later, but not in case of Windows XP operating systems. See the following link for more information: https://support.google.com/android/answer/182134.

Now that you have an understanding of how to enable USB tethering on an Android device, you'll explore in detail the internals of Android USB tethering. This chapter initially starts by exploring a brief picture of RNDIS specification and follows with a detailed explanation of how an Android tethering framework integrates itself within the Android USB framework. At end of the chapter, you'll explore how to use the USB tethering interface to reverse the tether that shares the network from the PC to an Android device.

RNDIS Specification Overview

Unlike other USB classes, RNDIS is not a USB class specification as defined by the USB implementer's forum, but is a Microsoft-specific network interface specification. According to Microsoft, the motivation behind this specification is to eliminate the need of vendor-specific network drivers. The role of the device is just to implement a transport driver that is complaint with RNDIS protocols. The RNDIS specification can be downloaded from the Microsoft web site using the following link: http://download.microsoft.com/download/B/0/B/B0B199DB-41E6-400F-90CD-C350D0C14A53/%5BMS-RNDIS%5D.pdf.

This specification defines communication protocols between a host and network devices connected over a transport such as a USB, thus enabling the host to have network connectivity. It is important to note that RNDIS specification does not define the transport to be used and its functionalities. The specification states that the transport bus has to provide reliable control and data channels for delivery network packets between the host and the device. Figure 4-3 illustrates the general architecture of the RNDIS protocol as provided by RNDIS specifications.

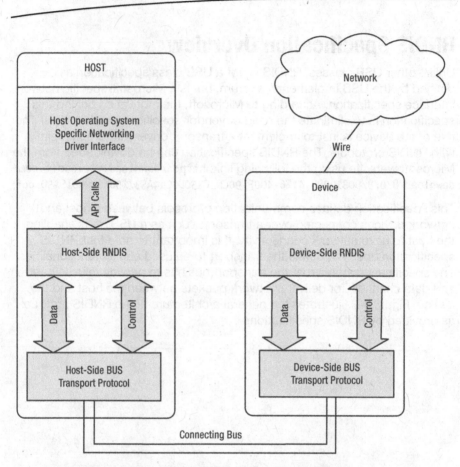

Figure 4-3. RNDIS protocol architechture (Ref: Figure 1 RNDIS Specification)

Figure 4-3 shows how the RNDIS protocol is placed above the transport protocol with a separate control and data channels. The control and data channel can be implemented by bulk and interrupt endpoints of the USB specification. Figure 4-4 illustrates interface and endpoints descriptors for an RNDIS function on an Android device.

```
Interface Descriptor:                                      Interface Descriptor:
  bLength          9                                         bLength          9
  bDescriptorType    4                                       bDescriptorType    4
  bInterfaceNumber   0                                       bInterfaceNumber   1
  bAlternateSetting  0                                       bAlternateSetting  0
  bNumEndpoints      1                                       bNumEndpoints      2
  bInterfaceClass    2 Communications                        bInterfaceClass    10 CDC Data
  bInterfaceSubClass  2 Abstract (modem)                     bInterfaceSubClass  0 Unused
  bInterfaceProtocol  255 Vendor Specific (MSFT RNDIS?)      bInterfaceProtocol  0
  iInterface         9 RNDIS Communications Control          iInterface          10 RNDIS Ethernet Data
  CDC Header:                                                Endpoint Descriptor:
    bcdCDC          1.10                                       bLength          7
  CDC Call Management:                                         bDescriptorType    5
    bmCapabilities   0x00                                      bEndpointAddress   0x81 EP 1 IN
    bDataInterface   1                                         bmAttributes       2
  CDC ACM:                                                      Transfer Type    Bulk
    bmCapabilities   0x00                                       Synch Type       None
  CDC Union:                                                    Usage Type       Data
    bMasterInterface  0                                        wMaxPacketSize    0x0200 1x 512 bytes
    bSlaveInterface   1                                        bInterval         0
  Endpoint Descriptor:                                      Endpoint Descriptor:
    bLength          7                                         bLength          7
    bDescriptorType    5                                       bDescriptorType    5
    bEndpointAddress   0x82 EP 2 IN                            bEndpointAddress   0x01 EP 1 OUT
    bmAttributes       3                                       bmAttributes       2
    Transfer Type    Interrupt                                 Transfer Type    Bulk
    Synch Type       None                                      Synch Type       None
    Usage Type       Data                                      Usage Type       Data
    wMaxPacketSize    0x0008 1x 8 bytes                        wMaxPacketSize    0x0200 1x 512 bytes
    bInterval        9                                         bInterval         0
```

Figure 4-4. RNDIS protocol interface descriptor

As mentioned earlier, RNDIS is Microsoft proprietary, not a defined protocol in the USB-IF's CDC specifications. However, an RNDIS function can use CDC with RNDIS as a vendor-defined protocol.

In the RNDIS Communications Control interface (bInterfaceNumber = 0), bInterfaceClass = 2 to specify a CDC interface. The bInterfaceSubclass field = 2 to specify the CDC Abstract Control Model subclass. The bInterfaceProtocol field = 255 to specify that the interface uses a vendor-defined protocol (RNDIS). The interface has one interrupt endpoint.

In the RNDIS Ethernet data interface (bInterfaceNumber = 1), bInterfaceClass = 10 to specify a CDC data interface. The interface has a bulk endpoint for each direction.

In this RNDIS setup, the responsibility of the host is to initialize the protocol, establish control and data channels with the Android device, and exchange control and data messages according to what the host operating system's network drivers need. The device's responsibility is to interpret the control messages sent by the host and respond to them with the appropriate data, indicating network and device status to the host and exchanging the data messages as requested by the host.

DO YOU KNOW?

Unlike the CDC's ECM subclass, RNDIS can combine multiple data packets and send them to the host in one single bus transfer, which can provide a better throughput performance.

Having seen a brief overview of the RNDIS specification, you'll now explore how this requirement is implemented inside the Android framework.

Android USB Tethering Framework

The Android tethering framework consists of multiple transports mechanisms, namely USB, WiFi, or Bluetooth, and this section focuses only on the framework that is involved in tethering over USB. Inside Android USB tethering, the transport layer is completely implemented inside the Android kernel. The Android USB framework provides the necessary infrastructure to enable tethering functionality in the Android kernel USB gadget driver. The USB gadget driver also registers itself to the kernel network driver to bring up a network interface over USB. When this USB Network interface is up, the Android connectivity framework takes control of the interface to manage network activity.

Android USB tethering implementation is spread over the USB Device manager and Connectivity Manager framework in the following files, respectively:

```
frameworks/base/services/java/com/android/server/usb/UsbDeviceManager.java
frameworks/base/services/java/com/android/server/connectivity/Tethering.java
frameworks/base/core/java/android/net/ConnectivityManager.java
frameworks/base/services/java/com/android/server/ConnectivityService.java
```

Figure 4-5 provides a top-level architecture view of Android USB tethering, illustrating USB and networking blocks.

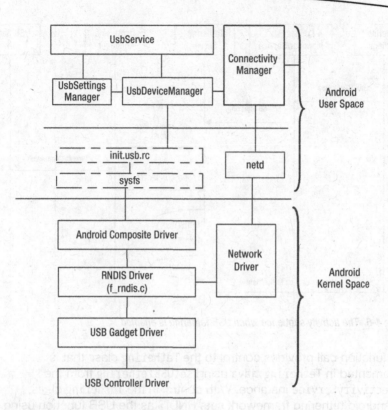

Figure 4-5. Android USB tethering architechture

The Android Connectivity framework uses the netd daemon present in /system/netd to manage the network interface for data service and to collect necessary statistics. Inside the kernel, the RNDIS USB gadget driver registers to the Linux network module as a USB Ethernet device.

Enabling USB Tethering

Now that you have an understanding of the internal blocks of USB tethering, this section explores how USB tethering is enabled inside Android framework. As explained in the initial section, USB tethering is enabled through the click of a checkbox under the Wireless and Networks settings. The USB tethering user interface is implemented through TetherSettings.java, which also handles updating state changes of USB tethering inside the Android framework using functions such as updateUsbState. When a user checks the USB tethering option, the click handler for the resource that is implemented invokes the setUSBTethering interface function, as shown in Figure 4-6.

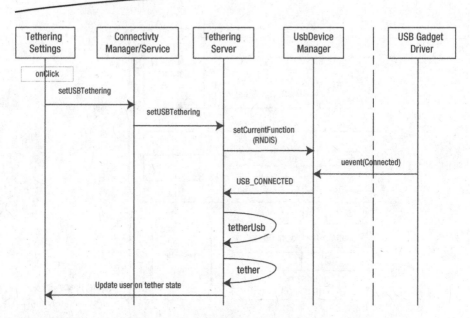

Figure 4-6. The activity sequence when USB tethering is enabled

This function call provides control to the Tethering class that is implemented in Tethering.java using setUSBTethering from the ConnectivityService.instance. With control in the Tethering class, the Android tethering framework sets RNDIS as the USB function using setCurrentFunction. This internally indicates to the USB kernel gadget driver to restart in RNDIS mode. Once the USB gadget driver is up, the kernel indicates to the Tethering class on the state change using uevents. This state change is used to start the connectivity management over the USB RNDIS network adapter, which is taken care of by tetherUSB function. Once the USB Ethernet interface is tethered, the status change is updated in the user interface.

Example: Reverse Tethering Over USB

In the previous section, we explored how the tethering of a data connection from an Android device is shared to a host PC. But there are times when providing an Internet connection of a host PC to an Android device is required. This example explains how to reverse a tether and share the Internet from a host PC to an Android device. You might need reverse tethering when you require a faster Internet connection (weak or no WiFi) or want to avoid the data charge of a 3G connection. Let's explore this for fun—this example requires a rooted Android device and was tried on an Ubuntu (12.04) Linux operating system with a rooted Samsung Tab2 with Cynogenmod.

Design and Flow

Reverse tether involves two key steps, namely, i) setting up the host PC to share an Internet connection, and ii) setting up the Android device to look for an Internet connection to the PC.

Host Setup

The host PC runs Ubuntu (12.04) and the steps for sharing an Internet connection are based on the link: https://help.ubuntu.com/community/ Internet/ConnectionSharing. The following snippet is a set of commands required to set up the Ubuntu host and is available as a script as part of the source code download located at http://www.apress.com/9781430262084.

```
echo 1 > /proc/sys/net/ipv4/ip_forward
ifconfig usb0 192.168.0.1 netmask 255.255.255.0 up
iptables -F
iptables -t nat -F
iptables -t nat -A POSTROUTING -o eth0 -j MASQUERADE
iptables -P FORWARD ACCEPT
```

```
usb0       Link encap:Ethernet  HWaddr 3e:7a:f7:2f:d0:45
           inet addr:192.168.0.1  Bcast:192.168.0.255  Mask:255.255.255.0
           inet6 addr: fe80::3c7a:f7ff:fe2f:d045/64 Scope:Link
           UP BROADCAST RUNNING MULTICAST  MTU:1500  Metric:1
           RX packets:138 errors:0 dropped:0 overruns:0 frame:0
           TX packets:160 errors:0 dropped:0 overruns:0 carrier:0
           collisions:0 txqueuelen:1000
           RX bytes:46835 (46.8 KB)  TX bytes:61611 (61.6 KB)
```

Device Setup

On the Android device, the requirement is to configure the network with the host PC as the gateway and also to provide generic DNS gateways. The following snippet is a set of commands that are required to set up the Android device and is available as a script at http://www.apress.com/9781430262084.

```
ifconfig rndis0 192.168.0.2 netmask 255.255.255.0 up
route add default gw 192.168.0.1 dev rndis0
setprop net.dns1 8.8.8.8
setprop net.dns2 8.8.4.4
```

```
root@android:/sdcard/Download # netcfg
netcfg
lo        UP                           127.0.0.1/8    0x00000049 00:00:00:00:00:00
ifb0      DOWN                           0.0.0.0/0    0x00000082 be:5d:8f:06:d0:81
ifb1      DOWN                           0.0.0.0/0    0x00000082 42:a2:ed:63:69:a6
sit0      DOWN                           0.0.0.0/0    0x00000080 00:00:00:00:00:00
ip6tnl0   DOWN                           0.0.0.0/0    0x00000080 00:00:00:00:00:00
rndis0    UP                         192.168.0.2/24   0x00001043 56:96:11:2f:1b:60
p2p0      UP                             0.0.0.0/0    0x00001003 be:20:a4:78:5e:e6
wlan0     UP                             0.0.0.0/0    0x00001003 bc:20:a4:78:5e:e6
root@android:/sdcard/Download # ifconfig rndis0
ifconfig rndis0
rndis0: ip 192.168.0.2 mask 255.255.255.0 flags [up broadcast running multicast]
```

Once both setups are successful, the Android device can use the Internet of the host PC. Figure 4-7 shows the configuration details and browses over the reverse tethered setup.

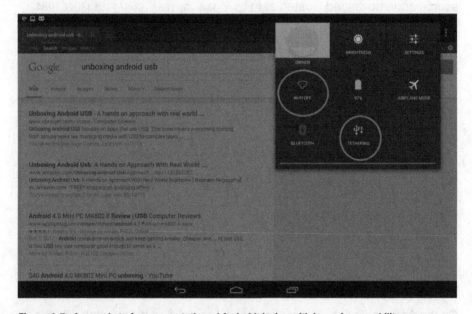

Figure 4-7. A snapshot of a reverse-tethered Android device with browsing capability

This device setup is automated as an application and is available as part of the source code download located at http://www.apress.com/9781430262084 and on https://git.techfugen.com/cgit/Android/apps/git/reverse_tether.git/.

There is also a script that is made available along with the Android source to help configure a host and an Android device in the following path: development/scripts/reverse_tether.sh. Though this example demonstrates reverse tethering on a Linux operating system, reverse tethering is also possible on Microsoft Windows and Apple's Mac operating systems.

## Chapter 5

USB Accessory

What you will learn:

- Android Open Accessory (AOA) Protocol
- USB HID Specification
- Android Open Accessory Framework
- Example: Android Open Accessory NFC Reader Using Cypress FX3

The Android Open Accessory protocol was introduced in Android Honeycomb version 3.1 and was also made available for the older 2.3.4 Gingerbread version. This was introduced to overcome the perceived limitation of Android-powered devices that cannot initiate connections with external USB devices. Android Open Accessory support is aimed at overcoming the limitation of not being able to initiate connection to external devices. Android-powered devices can now interact with Android accessories through the Android Open Accessory protocol. Figure 5-1 illustrates an Android accessory setup, showing how an Android accessory interacts with an Android-powered device.

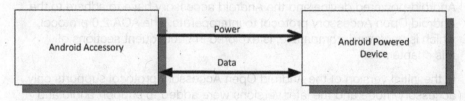

Figure 5-1. An Android accessory setup in accessory mode

Android accessories include items such as audio docks, lighting controllers, SLR camera controllers, and other products that a developer wants to communicate with over USB. In accessory mode, the Android-powered device functions as a USB device and the attached Android accessory functions as the USB host.

To facilitate developing accessory hardware, Google also introduced the Android Accessory Development Kit (ADK), a reference implementation of an Android Open Accessory device. This is aimed at helping Android hardware accessory builders and software developers create accessories for Android. Many chip manufacturers have come up with platforms based on this reference design to facilitate new product development.

This chapter focuses on the software aspect of Android Open Accessory (AOA), starting by exploring what is an Android Open Accessory protocol, which features are supported by it, and subsequently, how the protocol is placed in the Android USB framework with the help of block diagrams. The chapter also briefly discusses the USB HID (Human Interface Devices) specifications, which enable readers to effectively use Android Open Accessory 2.0 as it includes the HID feature. It is important to understand that the Android Open Accessory framework is spread across the Android user space and Android kernel. Information flows between these layers and is explored using sequence diagrams. At the end of this chapter, you'll explore these features with a case study example.

Android Open Accessory Protocol

As discussed, the Android Open Accessory (AOA) protocol was introduced in the Honeycomb version of Android. The Android Honeycomb version of the accessory protocol is referred to as AOA 1.0 and the equivalent development kit was named ADK 2011. The newer version AOA 2.0 of Android Open Accessory protocol was introduced as part of Android Jelly Bean with a supporting development kit referred as ADK 2012. Both the Android-powered device and the Android accessory have to adhere to the Android Open Accessory protocol to interoperate. The AOA 2.0 protocol, which is backward-compatible, is explored in subsequent sections of this chapter.

In the initial version of the Android Open Accessory protocol supports only accessory mode and the later versions were added to support audio and HID. Figure 5-2 illustrates the functions supported by the Android Open Accessory protocol.

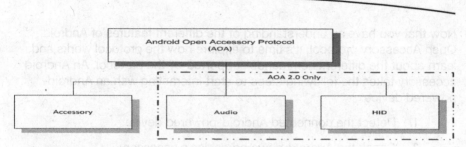

Figure 5-2. Features of the Android Open Accessory protocol

As illustrated in Figure 5-2, the AOA 2.0 protocol includes three unique features: accessory, audio, and HID.

ACCESSORY

An Android-powered device in accessory mode has a USB device port that uses two bulk endpoints. Bulk endpoints can transfer large amounts of data quickly but have no guaranteed maximum latency. The USB interface is exposed to the user space as a file for Android applications to perform data transfer between the Android-powered device and an Android accessory, which functions as the USB host.

AUDIO

The audio USB interface is new in Jelly Bean. It supports the standard USB 1.0 audio class so it can stream audio from an Android-powered device to an Android accessory.

HID

The HID feature is not exposed as a USB interface to the Android accessory. The HID feature is registered to an input subsystem of an Android-powered device through vendor-specific requests on the control endpoint. Once registered, an Android accessory can send inputs like key presses and cursor locations to an Android-powered device over USB. Note that in this example, the USB host sends key press and cursor data to the USB device, while with a conventional USB host, key press and cursor data travels from the device to the host.

Now that you have an understanding of the different features of Android Open Accessory protocol, it's time to explore how the protocol works and learn about the different commands supported by the protocol. An Android accessory takes the following steps to start interacting with an Android-powered device.

1. Detect the connected Android-powered device.

2. Check the Android-powered device's accessory mode.

3. Set the necessary mode settings and start the Android-powered device in accessory mode.

4. Start communicating with the Android-powered device. In some cases, the Android-powered device must have an application that can understand and respond to the Android accessory's communications.

When enumerated successfully in accessory mode, an Android-powered device uses a product ID based on the supported functionality. Only the first two product IDs are applicable in the AOA 1.0 version. After enumerating in accessory mode, the Android-powered device uses Google's vendor ID of 0x18d1.

```
0x2D00 - accessory
0x2D01 - accessory + adb
0x2D02 - audio
0x2D03 - audio + adb
0x2D04 - accessory + audio
0x2D05 - accessory + audio + adb
```

Having studied how the accessory hardware enumerates an Android-powered device in accessory mode, you'll now explore the USB control request and the requests used. Requests related to audio functions will not be discussed in the following section, but you can refer to Chapter 6, "USB Audio," which details the USB audio specification along with audio device and host functions.

The accessory protocol operates on the control endpoint (endpoint 0) using the vendor extension option provided by the USB control requests. The following section describes the format of these vendor-specific control requests, which manage the accessory protocol. Later sections explain how these requests can be used.

Getting Accessory Protocol Version

This control request is used to determine the protocol version supported by the Android-powered device. The request code is 51 and is indicated through the bRequest field in the Setup packet of the control request. When this request is received, the Android-powered device sends the supported protocol version. When the device supports the AOA 1.0 protocol, it returns 1 in the data stage of the control transfer, and when the device supports AOA 2.0, it returns 2 in the data stage.

bmRequestType	bRequest	wValue	wIndex	wLength	Data
DEVICE_TO_HOST | TYPE_VENDOR	ACCESSORY_GET_ PROTOCOL (51)	0	0	2	1 when AOA 1.0 2 when AOA 2.0

Managing HID

To manage the HID function in accessory mode, multiple control requests are required. They can register/unregister the function and initiate HID events. The following section explains these control requests.

The request ACCESSORY_REGISTER_HID with code 54 is used to hook the accessory HID to the input system of the Android-powered device. This request also holds information about the length of the report descriptor, which will be subsequently sent, and also assigns an ID for future communication.

bmRequestType	bRequest	wValue	wIndex	wLength	Data
HOST_TO_DEVICE | TYPE_VENDOR	ACCESSORY_ REGISTER_HID (54)	Accessory assigned ID for the HID device	Length of the HID report descriptor	0	None

The protocol also allows an accessory to unhook the registered HID using the ACCESSORY_UNREGISTER_HID request with a request code of 55. The ID parameter should be the same one that was used during the register command.

bmRequestType	bRequest	wValue	wIndex	wLength	Data
HOST_TO_DEVICE | TYPE_VENDOR	ACCESSORY_ UNREGISTER_HID (55)	Accessory assigned ID for the HID device	0	0	None

Once the HID is hooked up, the input system of the Android accessory can send HID report data to the Android-powered device. The command, ACCESSORY_SEND_HID_EVENT with request code 57, enables the Android accessory to send a HID report to the Android-powered device using the ID assigned during registration.

bmRequestType	bRequest	wValue	wIndex	wLength	Data
HOST_TO_DEVICE | TYPE_VENDOR	ACCESSORY_ SEND_HID_ EVENT (57)	Accessory assigned ID for the HID device	0	Length of data	HID report for the event

Whenever the HID report data is larger than the maximum data supported by the control endpoint, the Android accessory should use the following request to send the remaining data. The wIndex parameter holds the offset, which should be used to concatenate the data.

bmRequestType	bRequest	wValue	wIndex	wLength	Data
HOST_TO_DEVICE | TYPE_VENDOR	ACCESSORY_SET_ HID_REPORT_ DESC (56)	Accessory assigned ID for the HID device	Offset of data in descriptor	Length of data	HID report descriptor

Switching to Accessory Mode

When an Android accessory finishes collecting information and setting up the Android-powered device for accessory mode, it uses the request ACCESSORY_START with code 51. This request triggers the Android-powered device to switch to accessory mode, which means the device re-enumerates with Google's vendor ID and a product ID based on the enabled feature.

bmRequestType	bRequest	wValue	wIndex	wLength	Data
HOST_TO_DEVICE | TYPE_VENDOR	ACCESSORY_START (53)	0	0	0	None

Informational Requests

This request sends descriptive information from the Android accessory to the Android-powered device. The Android-powered device can display the strings returned by the Android accessory to the user. The Android accessory uses requests with code 52 to send the string information.

bmRequestType	bRequest	wValue	wIndex	wLength	Data
HOST_TO_DEVICE | TYPE_VENDOR	ACCESSORY_SEND_ STRING (52)	0	String ID	Length of string	Null-terminated UTF-8 string

The following are the string types that the Android accessory may send to the Android-powered device. The wIndex field of the request specifies the string type.

```
#define ACCESSORY_STRING_MANUFACTURER   0
#define ACCESSORY_STRING_MODEL          1
#define ACCESSORY_STRING_DESCRIPTION    2
#define ACCESSORY_STRING_VERSION        3
#define ACCESSORY_STRING_URI            4
#define ACCESSORY_STRING_SERIAL         5
```

Now that you've seen various commands supported by the accessory protocol, you can move to the next section, which briefly explores the USB HID specification, as AOA 2.0 supports HID as one of its features.

USB HID Specification

Human Interface Devices (HIDs) are devices that are used primarily by people to control the operation of computer systems. Typical examples for HID-class devices include keyboards, mice, joysticks, and barcode readers. The USB Human Interface Device (HID) class specification defines a standard way for HIDs to communicate with a host that supports the HID class.

Figure 5-3 illustrates different USB pipes involved in a typical USB HID setup that pass information from the device to a host. A control endpoint is used to receive and respond to USB-related control and class information, and an interrupt endpoint is used to transmit asynchronous data.

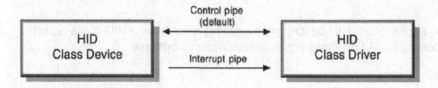

Figure 5-3. A typical USB HID setup

These pipes are exposed as descriptors to a USB host. Figure 5-4 illustrates the descriptor tree of a typical USB HID device. As you can see from the descriptor tree, it is similar to any other USB device, with the exception of the additional HID descriptor information.

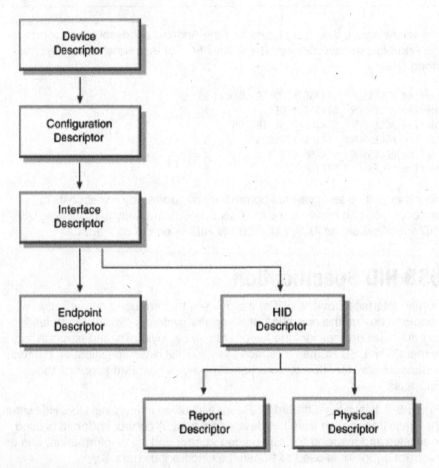

Figure 5-4. Descriptor tree of a simple USB HID device

In addition to a HID descriptor, every HID must have a HID-class report descriptor. A HID-class physical descriptor is optional.

PHYSICAL DESCRIPTOR

A *physical descriptor* is a collection of information that describes a specific part or parts of the human body that will manage the control or controls in the HID device. This descriptor is optional and adds complexity to the complete system. This section does not go into much detail about the physical descriptor, as it is rarely used and is not used in the accessory protocol.

Report Descriptor

A *report descriptor* contains a collection of information that describes the data that a HID sends and receives. Each piece of information in a report descriptor is an "item" that consists of a byte that identifies the item and one or more bytes that contain the item's data. For example, 0x15 is the Logical Minimum item, and a value of 0x00 sets the logical minimum value of the item to 0x00. A standard format for items is used, as illustrated in Figure 5-5.

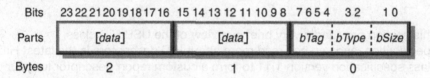

Figure 5-5. Report descriptor item format

The item field is classified into types based on the first byte fields, namely:

- bSize: These two bits differentiate whether an item is a short or long item, thereby indicating the length of data in the item.

- bType: These bits classify an item as Main, Global, or Local type. These types help to define the meanings of the data in the report.

- bTag: These bits specify the function of the item and will vary for each type of item.

During enumeration, the USB host requests the report descriptor from a HID class device. The host uses the information in the report descriptor to parse the data in received HID reports, as illustrated in Figure 5-6. Figure 5-6 is a very simple representation of a report descriptor, but in a practical setup, the usage and collections are nested to provide relevant details.

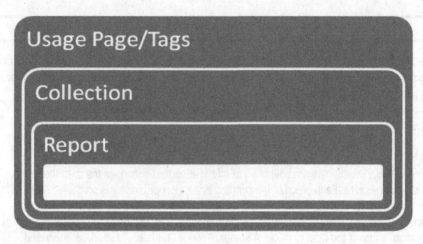

Figure 5-6. A HID report descriptor

This section provided a very brief overview of the USB HID class specification, and you can read more about HID descriptors in the latest HID class specification version 1.11 to form a custom report descriptor for your accessory device.

Android Open Accessory Framework

The Android Open Accessory (AOA) framework provides the necessary interface for a user to manage and interact with an Android accessory. The Android USB accessory framework acts as a responder, and primarily responds to an Android accessory, which initiates the communication with an Android-powered device to switch to accessory mode. The responder implementation of the Android USB accessory framework is spread across roughly three major files: `frameworks/base/services/java/com/android/server/usb/UsbDeviceManager.java`, `frameworks/base/services/java/com/android/server/usb/UsbService.java`, and `/frameworks/base/services/jni/com_android_server_UsbDeviceManager.cpp`.

This Android framework is exposed via APIs as implemented in `/frameworks/base/core/java/android/hardware/usb/UsbAccessory.java`.

Various accessory-related constants discussed in the previous section are defined in `external/kernel-headers/original/linux/usb/f_accessory.h`.

Having seen how different the code of the Android USB accessory framework is organized within the Android framework, you'll now explore the building blocks of the Android USB Accessory framework. Figure 5-7 illustrates the architecture of the Android Open Accessory (AOA) framework from the Android kernel to the Android framework in the user space.

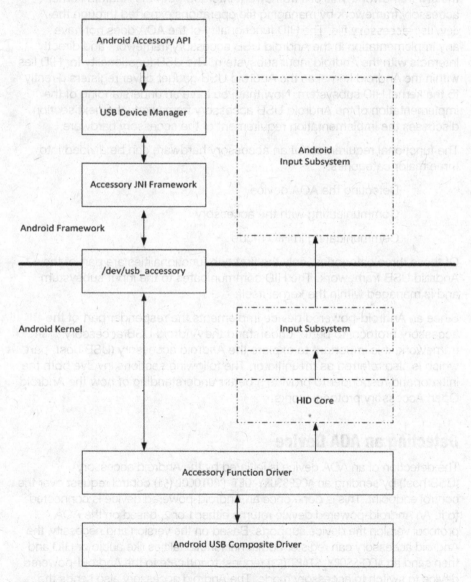

Figure 5-7. The architecture of Android Open Accessory 2.0 (AOA 2.0) framework

From Figure 5-7, it is apparent that most of the AOA framework is in the kernel space and the interface to the user space is through file operations. The AOA framework implementation in user space is mixed with the USB Manager implementation that manages the USB states of the Android-powered device. The other part of the AOA implementation is part of the JNI framework. This JNI framework interacts with the Android kernel accessory framework by managing file operations exported through the /dev/usb_accessory file. The HID functionality of the AOA does not have any implementation in the Android USB accessory framework and directly interacts with the Android input subsystem. The USB functionality for HID lies within the Android kernel as the Android USB gadget driver registers directly to the kernel HID subsystem. Now that you have an understanding of the implementation of the Android USB accessory framework, the next section discusses the implementation requirement of the accessory hardware.

The functional requirement of an accessory hardware can be divided into three major categories:

- Detecting the AOA device

- Communicating with the accessory

- Communicating in HID mode

Of these three categories, only the first two functionalities are part of the Android USB framework. The HID communicates to the input subsystem and is managed within the kernel itself.

Since an Android-powered device implements the responder part of the accessory protocol to better understand the Android USB accessory framework, it is important to explore the Android accessory (USB host) part, which is also referred as the initiator. The following sections involve both the initiator and responder to provide a better understanding of how the Android Open Accessory protocol works.

Detecting an AOA Device

The detection of an AOA device is initiated by the Android accessory (USB host) by sending an ACCESSORY_GET_PROTOCOL (51) control request over the control endpoint. This is done once an Android-powered device is connected to it. An Android-powered device returns either 1 or 2, based on the AOA protocol version the device supports. Based on the version and necessity, the Android accessory can register additional functionalities like audio or HID and then send an ACCESSORY_START (53) request to indicate to the Android-powered device to switch to accessory mode. The Android accessory also sends the ACCESSORY_SEND_STRING (52) request to provide the manufacturer, model, and version strings before sending the ACCESSORY_START request.

This next section explains the control and data flow that happens within the Android USB framework of an Android-powered device. Communication to the Android USB framework starts only when the Android-powered device receives the ACCESSORY_START (53) request. Requests like ACCESSORY_GET_PROTOCOL (51) are responded to and from the kernel layer, as illustrated in Figure 5-8. When ACCESSORY_START (53) is received, the kernel layer sends a UEvent indicating that it has received the request to switch to accessory mode. To detect this information flow from the Android kernel to the UsbDeviceManager framework (as discussed in Chapter 2), the UsbDeviceManager framework registers the Android framework to monitor UEvent changes with the string "DEVPATH=/devices/virtual/misc/usb_accessory", as shown here:

```
private static final String ACCESSORY_START_MATCH =
        "DEVPATH=/devices/virtual/misc/usb_accessory";

mUEventObserver.startObserving(ACCESSORY_START_MATCH);
```

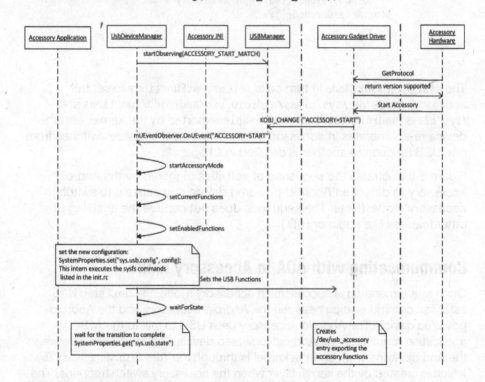

Figure 5-8. The Android Open Accessory detection sequence

When the UEventObserver matches the particular registered string, the observer module that registered for the UEvent is notified, and in this case, it is the UsbDeviceManager framework. The following snippet from UsbDeviceManager.java implements the onUEvent, which receives the notification and decodes the information in order to decide on the accessory mode, subsequently calling startAccessoryMode when it is in accessory mode.

```
private final UEventObserver mUEventObserver = new UEventObserver() {
@Override
public void onUEvent(UEventObserver.UEvent event) {
if (DEBUG) Slog.v(TAG, "USB UEVENT: " + event.toString());

    String state = event.get("USB_STATE");
    String accessory = event.get("ACCESSORY");
    if (state != null) {
            mHandler.updateState(state);
    } else if ("START".equals(accessory)) {
            if (DEBUG) Slog.d(TAG, "got accessory start");
            startAccessoryMode();
    }
}
};
```

The startAccessoryMode in turn calls setCurrentFunctions to set the accessory mode via /sys/class/android_usb/android0/functions and /sys/class/android_usb/android0/enable exported by the kernel, and the device re-enumerates in accessory mode. The way the device switches from one USB function to another is detailed in Chapter 2.

Figure 5-8 illustrates the sequence of activities triggered by the Android accessory to detect an Android-powered device and cause it to switch to accessory mode. (Note: The sequence does not capture the enabling of other features like audio or HID.)

Communicating with AOA in Accessory Mode

Once re-enumeration is successful in accessory mode, the next step is to establish communication between the Android accessory and the Android-powered device. The Android accessory uses USB to talk to the AOA application running on the Android-powered device. Communication between the Android framework and the kernel is through the /dev/usb_accessory file, which is created by the kernel layer when the accessory switch happens. The file is created in the /dev directory and is managed by the JNI implementation com_android_server_UsbDeviceManager.cpp, as defined:

```
#define DRIVER_NAME "/dev/usb_accessory"
```

Android provides APIs to directly manage this file from the application through this JNI implementation. The following sequence diagram (Figure 5-9) provides an overview of the communication flow between the Android AOA framework and the Android kernel (implemented in drivers/usb/gadget/ f_accessory.c), along with the accessory hardware.

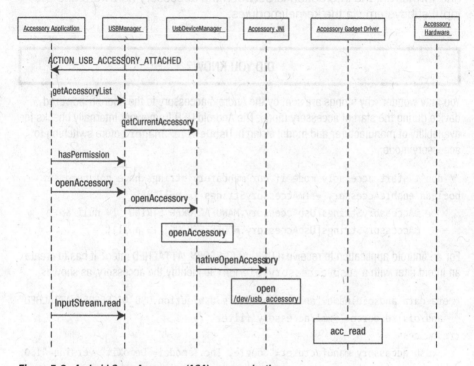

Figure 5-9. Android Open Accessory (AOA) communication

Whenever an application invokes an openAccessory API from the UsbDeviceManager, a native function call implemented in the JNI framework is invoked. Once the open operation is successful, normal read, write, and ioctl operations can be done using the file descriptor returned by the openAccessory function.

Registering and Communicating in HID Mode

A typical Android accessory setup might require small amounts of data such as key events (volume control, setting up time, and so on) or others that are similar and are appropriate for the HID class. The AOA protocol uses vendor-specific requests over the control endpoint to simulate HID class communications. This section explains how to register a HID function in accessory mode and transfer data from an Android accessory to an Android device.

When an Android-powered device is in accessory mode and is functioning as a HID, the complete functionality lies within the kernel, with the accessory gadget driver directly interacting with the HID core kernel module. The HID core further interacts with the input subsystem of the Android framework. The Android USB framework is involved only to switch into accessory mode, and further on, the interaction is between the accessory hardware and the input subsystem via the kernel modules.

 DID YOU KNOW?

You may wonder why strings are sent by the Android accessory to the Android-powered device during the start of accessory mode. The Android USB framework internally checks for availability of manufacturer and model string in `UsbDeviceManager` before switching to accessory mode:

```
// don't start accessory mode if our mandatory strings have not been set
boolean enableAccessory = (mAccessoryStrings != null &&
        mAccessoryStrings[UsbAccessory.MANUFACTURER_STRING] != null &&
        mAccessoryStrings[UsbAccessory.MODEL_STRING] != null);
```

For an Android application to receive a USB_ACCESSORY_ATTACHED intent, it has to create an intent filter with a `<usb-accessory>`element to identify the accessory, as shown.

```
<meta-data android:name="android.hardware.usb.action.USB_ACCESSORY_ATTACHED"
    android:resource="@xml/accessory_filter" />
<resources>
    <usb-accessory manufacturer="Google, Inc." model="DemoKit" version="1.0"
/>
</resources>
```

Figure 5-10 illustrates how to register a HID function in accessory mode and transfer a HID report.

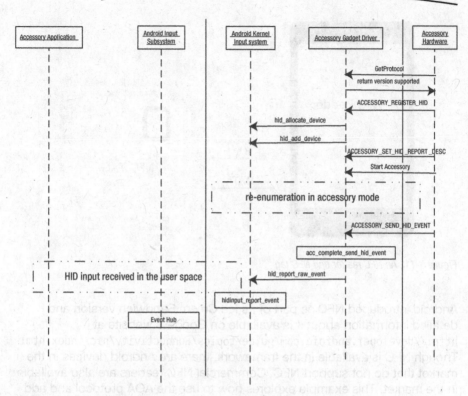

Figure 5-10. Android Open Accessory HID registration and communication process

In the previous sections, you explored the Android accessory framework. The following section demonstrates how to use this framework with an example that interacts with an NFC device to convert the Android-powered device to an NFC reader using the accessory interface.

Example: Android Open Accessory NFC Reader Using Cypress Fx3

Near field communication (NFC) is a communication protocol that facilitates communication between two devices mainly in a mobile ecosystem. NFC extends on the Radio Frequency Identification (RFID) technology and operates at a frequency of 13.56MHz. In an NFC environment, two entities are involved in the transaction—a reader (initiator) and a tag (responder). Figure 5-11 illustrates a simple NFC reader and tag.

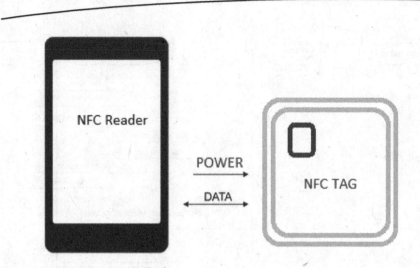

Figure 5-11. An NFC reader and NFC tag

Android introduced NFC as part of its Ice Cream Sandwich version and detailed information about it is available on Google's website at http://developer.android.com/guide/topics/connectivity/nfc/index.html. Though NFC is available in the framework, there are Android devices in the market that do not support NFC. Commercial NFC readers are also available in the market. This example explores how to use the AOA protocol and add external NFC reader capabilities to an Android device. Figure 5-12 provides the setup details.

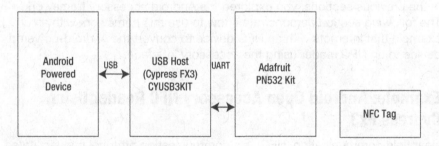

Figure 5-12. An NFC reader and NFC tag setup

Design and Flow

Figure 5-13 captures the flow of activities in the setup shown in Figure 5-12, which is used to retrieve a tag's basic information.

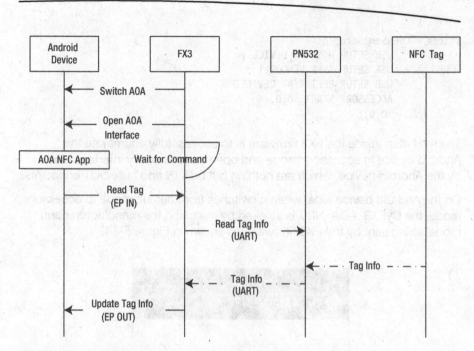

Figure 5-13. Sequence of activities in AOA NFC reader setup

The first step in the process is to connect the PN532 NFC shield board to the Cypress FX3 development kit over a UART interface and place a tag, say a Mifare card, near the PN532 NFC shield board. Once the setup is ready, you power up the FX3 board and load the AOA NFC firmware. (Refer to the Cypress documentation for how to set this up at http://www.cypress.com/?rID=57990.) This should boot up the FX3 board in USB host mode.

On the Android device, you install the CyFX3_AOA_NFC application and connect the Android device to the FX3 board using an OTG cable. When the FX3 board detects a device insertion, it initiates the accessory protocol and switches the Android device to accessory mode.

```
sendString( ACCESSORY_STRING_MANUFACTURER, "Cypress");

sendString(ACCESSORY_STRING_MODEL, "FX3 NFC Reader");

sendString( ACCESSORY_STRING_DESCRIPTION, "FX3 Android Accessory NFC Reader");

sendString(ACCESSORY_STRING_VERSION, "0.1");

sendString(ACCESSORY_STRING_URI, "www.cypress.com");

sendString(ACCESSORY_STRING_SERIAL, "0123456789");
```

```
status = CyFxSendSetupRqt(
            USB_SETUP_HOST_TO_DEVICE |
            USB_SETUP_TYPE_VENDOR |
            USB_SETUP_RECIPIENT_DEVICE,
            ACCESSORY_START, 0,0,
             0,0);
```

The next step inside the FX3 firmware is to successfully enumerate the Android device in accessory mode and open the accessory interface shared by the Android device, which are nothing but bulk IN and bulk OUT endpoints.

On the Android device side, when it switches from default mode to accessory mode, the CyFX3_AOA_NFC is invoked by matching the manufacturer and model string sent by the FX3 firmware, as shown in Figure 5-14.

Figure 5-14. Snapshot of the CyFX3_AOA_NFC application

Now press the Read TAG button to initiate the tag-reading process. Internally this will send a custom command over the IN endpoint to the FX3. The FX3 firmware recognizes that the application has asked for tag

information. To get the tag information, the FX3 firmware sends a sequence
of commands (shown next) specific to the PN532 NFC shield board over the
UART interface, as shown in the Figure 5-13.

```
/*To wake-up the PN532 NFC Reader */
send: 55 55 00 00 00 00 00 00 00 00 00 00 00 00 00 00 ff 03 fd d4 14 01 17
00
return: 00 00 FF 00 FF 00 00 00 FF 02 FE D5 15 16 00

/*To read the NFC Tag information. Bytes XX holds the TAG information*/
send: 00 00 FF 04 FC D4 4A 01 00 E1 00
return: 00 00 FF 00 FF 00 00 00 FF 0C F4 D5 4B 01 01 00 04 08 04 XX XX XX XX
5A 00
```

The PN532 NFC shield returns the tag information, which is read over the
UART, back to the FX3 firmware. The FX3 firmware subsequently sends
back the tag information over the OUT endpoint to the Android device
in accessory mode. The information is displayed in the edit box of the
application as shown in the Figure 5-15

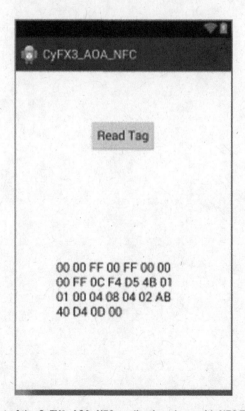

Figure 5-15. Snapshot of the CyFX3_AOA_NFC application along with NFC Tag info

Conclusion

The Android Open Accessory (AOA) protocol extends the power of Android-powered devices by allowing the device to manage and communicate to external hardware in device mode. For developers, there are many platform providers who can provide accessory hardware development kits that enable developers to experiment and come up with new ideas. You can find many interesting videos about Android open accessories on YouTube. The official video from Google that presents the AOA protocol can be found at http://www.youtube.com/watch?v=s7szcpXf2rE.

The following links provide relevant information about Android Open Accessory protocols: http://developer.android.com/tools/adk/index.html and http://source.android.com/tech/accessories/index.html, which contain an official description of the protocol. You can also find reference implementations of the accessory software and hardware in following Git repository: https://android.googlesource.com/device/google/accessory/adk2012_demo.

## Chapter 6

USB Audio

What you will learn:

- USB Audio Specification
- Android USB Audio
  - USB Host Audio
    - Playing Audio Over a USB Headset from an Android Device
  - USB Device Audio
    - Android Accessory Audio Dock Using Cypress FX3

Entertainment is a key feature that users look for in any mobile device when making a purchase decision. Android is no different in this regard, and it addresses this issue with enriched features to entertain end users. Google's online digital store, Google Play, provides access to music, books, movies, and apps to entertain the user. When it comes to music or movies, audio is a key aspect that makes a huge difference in the user experience. To experience quality audio, it is important to have a better transport mechanism to move the audio data from the Android-powered device to an external device. Android uses digital interfaces like USB, HDMI, and Bluetooth as transport mechanisms to stream and move the audio data around. Though there are different transport mechanisms, this chapter explores USB as the audio transport interface.

Before starting, you must understand the different USB audio accessories available in the market. The USB-based audio accessories can be broadly classified based on the USB mode (host or device mode). Remember, there are other audio accessories that use USB connections to stream audio. These are referred as analog accessories and do not comply with USB specification, thus they don't fall into the USB mode classification.

ANALOG USB AUDIO

Audio accessories that use USB interfaces to stream audio data and follow the (obsolete) USB Carkit n Specification (CEA-936-A) are generally referred to as analog audio systems. When streaming analog data, these devices use only the physical interface of USB and do not comply with USB specifications.

USB HOST AUDIO

In the market, there are Android devices (like tablet PCs) that can function as USB hosts and are capable of communicating with USB devices connected to them. These Android devices can support USB headsets to play back music and perform other audio functions. Though not officially supported by Android CDD (Compatibility Definition Document), this chapter explores these devices before moving onto device audio.

USB DEVICE AUDIO

Android-powered devices acting in USB accessory mode are mandated to support an audio interface as one of its accessory interfaces by Android CDD. Introduced in the Jelly Bean version of Android, this feature enables vendors to come up with new types of accessories that can receive audio stream from an Android device through USB and play it back to the users. Though there are not many devices available in the market except what was demonstrated in Google I/O 2012 (by Gear4), the later half of this chapter explores how to build this accessory audio device.

Now that you've read a quick overview of the different USB audio devices available in the market, let's explore how the Android framework accommodates the later two USB audio device types within an Android-powered device. To understand the Android framework, it's important to understand USB audio. The following section provides a brief overview of the USB audio specification.

USB Audio Specification

The USB audio class specification provides a standard mechanism to transport audio over USB, and this section is based on the USB-IF's device class definition for audio devices, Release 1.0. The USB audio specification allows audio devices to interoperate by making software drivers as generic as possible. Like any other USB device, USB audio devices use descriptors to describe their characteristics to a host. These descriptors hold detailed information about the audio device, including information about how to control and stream digital audio. But unlike other USB classes like Mass Storage Class (MSC) or MTP, where the descriptors are more or less fixed, a USB audio device descriptor varies based on the topology of the product. This is because most of the features are optional and vendors can build an audio device with multiple functionalities, thus the descriptor tree varies between devices.

An audio device exposes its functionality to a host through its interfaces, namely the audio control `interface`Audio streaming interface and the midi streaming interface. An audio function must have at least one audio control interface; the streaming interfaces are optional. A collection of single control interfaces and sets of streaming interfaces is called an "audio interface collection." Figure 6-1 represents an audio function with different interfaces, as illustrated in the USB audio class specification.

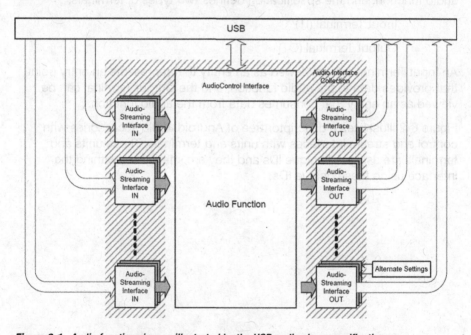

Figure 6-1. Audio function view as illustrated by the USB audio class specification

In simple terms, the audio control interface is used to manage functionality that directly influences audio perception, including volume control, and the audio streaming interface is mainly used to transport audio data between the audio function and the external world.

To manage the properties of an audio function, the USB audio class specification represents the audio function as addressable entities, namely terminals and units. *Units* form the building blocks of an audio function, representing sub-functionality of the USB function. These are the five standard units as defined by the USB audio specification:

- Mixer Unit (MU)
- Selector Unit (SU)
- Feature Unit (FU)
- Processing Unit (PU)
- Extension Unit (XU)

Each unit manages a certain functionality of the audio function and is associated with a unit descriptor, which can identify and describe the characteristics of the unit. A *terminal* represents the connection points of an audio function, and the specification defines two types of terminals:

- Input Terminal (IT)
- Output Terminal (OT)

An Input Terminal can be viewed as an entity that represents an entry point that provides data to the audio function, and the Output Terminal can be viewed as an entity that consumes data from the audio function.

Figure 6-2 illustrates a descriptor tree of Android audio accessories with control and stream interfaces with units and terminals. These units and terminals are assigned unique IDs and they are interlinked, withing the interface using these unique IDs.

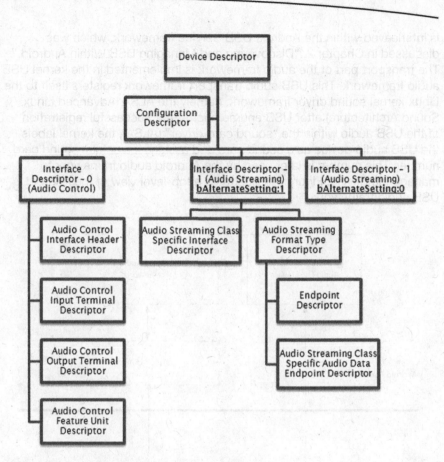

Figure 6-2. Descriptor tree of an Android audio accessory

The unique ID is also used to address a particular entity for which an audio control request is to be sent. These requests are used to control the functionality and characteristics of the audio function, such as volume control and mute, among others.

Having been briefed on the USB audio specification, you'll now explore the building blocks of the Android USB framework and also explore how the Android USB framework interfaces with the Android audio framework when in USB host and device modes.

Android USB Audio

The Android USB audio framework is very thin when compared to other Android USB frameworks, and it does not have dedicated files or directories in which the functionality is implemented. Android USB audio functionality is interleaved within the Android USB Service framework, which was discussed in Chapter 2, "Discovering and Managing USB Within Android." The transport part of the audio framework is implemented in the kernel USB audio framework. This USB audio transport framework registers itself to the Linux kernel sound driver framework, namely the ALSA (Advanced Linux Sound Architecture) after USB enumeration. After successful registration of the USB audio within the "sound card driver" (ALSA), the kernel labels the USB audio device as a sound card and assigns it a unique sound card number. This number is later used by the Android audio framework to manage the device. Figure 6-3 illustrates a top-level view of the Android USB audio framework.

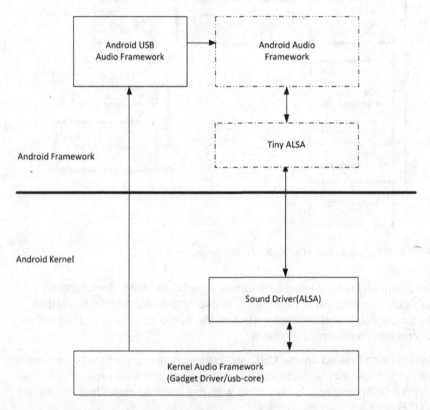

Figure 6-3. Android USB audio architechtural view

The architecture of the USB device audio and USB host audio setup remains the same. The only difference between these two is that in a USB device setup, the kernel driver is the gadget driver module, and in a host setup, the USB device connected is managed by the usb-core kernel module, as illustrated in Figure 6-3.

The Android USB audio framework is interleaved within the Android USB Service framework, which just detects the USB functionality and generates appropriate "intent" in order to pass the information to the Android audio framework and indicate availability of a USB audio device. To understand the simple framework of Android USB audio functionality, you have to explore how the Android USB Service framework detects and communicates USB audio device information to the Android audio framework. The following sections explain intents that communicate detection of a USB audio device and how these USB audio intents are generated and broadcasted along with the sound card information.

Different audio output devices supported by the Android framework are defined in frameworks/base/media/java/android/media/AudioManager.java. The following code snippet shows the constants used to define USB audio devices from the Android audio manager framework:

```
/** {@hide} The audio output device code for a USB audio accessory.
 * The accessory is in USB host mode and the
   Android device in USB device mode
*/
public static final int DEVICE_OUT_USB_ACCESSORY = AudioSystem.DEVICE_OUT_
USB_ACCESSORY;

/** {@hide} The audio output device code for a USB audio device. The device
is in USB device mode and the Android device in USB host mode
 */
public static final int DEVICE_OUT_USB_DEVICE = AudioSystem.DEVICE_OUT_USB_
DEVICE;
```

This audio device output code information is used by the Android audio framework as part of policy decisions, such as routing the audio data. The comments above each definition explain which USB audio device the definition represents.

To communicate detection of these USB output devices, two intents are used. These intents are defined in a common Android framework file, named frameworks/base/core/java/android/content/Intent.java. The two USB audio intents, when broadcast, carry device and sound card information created by the USB device. This information is necessary for the audio framework to further manage the audio device. Next, we'll explore the details of the two intents.

Intent for DEVICE_OUT_USB_ACCESSORY

When an Android-powered device acts as a USB device and goes into USB audio accessory mode, the following intent is generated along with the device and sound card information created by the USB device.

```
/**
 * Broadcast Action: A USB audio accessory was plugged in or unplugged.
 *
 * <p>The intent will have the following extra values:
 * <ul>
 *    <li><em>state</em> - 0 for unplugged, 1 for plugged. </li>
 *    <li><em>card</em> - ALSA card number (integer) </li>
 *    <li><em>device</em> - ALSA device number (integer) </li>
 * </ul>
 * </ul>
 * @hide
 */
@SdkConstant(SdkConstantType.BROADCAST_INTENT_ACTION)
public static final String ACTION_USB_AUDIO_ACCESSORY_PLUG =
        "android.intent.action.USB_AUDIO_ACCESSORY_PLUG";
```

Intent for DEVICE_OUT_USB_DEVICE

An Android device with a USB host port can attach to a USB audio device like a USB headset. In this case, the following intent is generated along with device and sound card information created for the USB device.

```
/**
 * Broadcast Action: A USB audio device was plugged in or unplugged.
 *
 * <p>The intent will have the following extra values:
 * <ul>
 *    <li><em>state</em> - 0 for unplugged, 1 for plugged. </li>
 *    <li><em>card</em> - ALSA card number (integer) </li>
 *    <li><em>device</em> - ALSA device number (integer) </li>
 * </ul>
 * </ul>
 * @hide
 */
@SdkConstant(SdkConstantType.BROADCAST_INTENT_ACTION)
public static final String ACTION_USB_AUDIO_DEVICE_PLUG =
        "android.intent.action.USB_AUDIO_DEVICE_PLUG";
```

USB Host Audio

When an Android device such as a tablet PC, has a USB host port and supports USB host mode, one of the key USB functionalities a user expects is to have playback over a USB-powered audio device. Though Android CDD doesn't mandate and support USB host audio, the Android framework has added stubs to enable this feature for future expansion. For example, the USB_AUDIO_DEVICE_PLUG intent is defined but not generated in Jelly Bean. This section explores a possible way to work around this, by giving the Android Audio framework a new sound card created by the USB audio device.

Since the Android USB framework does not implement USB host audio, there is no source file to refer to in the Android USB framework for this functionality. The stubs like the USB_AUDIO_DEVICE_PLUG intent's definition are available in frameworks/base/core/java/android/content/Intent.java, as explained in the previous section. The Android audio service framework also provides a stub of receiving the intent when it is broadcasted.

It is also important to know that in the USB host audio use case, most of the USB-related work is done at the kernel level (usb-core and sound driver ALSA), and the rest is taken care of in the Android audio framework, along with user space ALSA. The link /proc/asound/cards, as shown in Figure 6-4, is not available yet in the Android USB framework, but does have the essential information for the intent generated by the Android USB Service Manager framework. Figure-6-4 illustrates a typical USB host mode audio architecture.

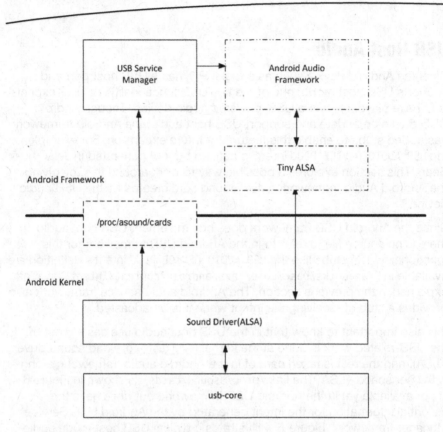

Figure 6-4. Android USB host audio architecture

As shown in Figure 6-4, the kernel audio driver implementation ALSA is part of the sound/usb folder of the kernel package. Whenever an audio device is plugged into an Android-powered device, the usbcore manages the USB audio device enumeration and registers the audio device to the ALSA layer. Through the kernel-level ALSA layer and equivalent user space ALSA libraries, the Android audio framework manages the USB audio device for playback and other features.

In the typical Linux system and Android 4.0 and below, there is a user space with ALSA as well. But with the Jelly Bean version of Android, a lightweight user space ALSA library named tinyalsa has been introduced in order to enable the Android audio framework to manage the audio devices connected in a lightweight fashion. It is important to note that the ability to support USB audio with playback or voice depends on the Android audio framework and ALSA. The USB framework in audio use cases is just a transport layer passing data from the audio framework to the DAC in real time.

Now that you've read a brief overview of the USB host audio, the next section explores a workaround you can use to give the Android audio framework a new sound card created by the USB audio device.

Example: How to Play Audio Over a USB Headset from an Android Device

As discussed in the previous section, in a USB host audio use case, an Android device has all the necessary framework from the USB transport to the Android audio framework. The missing link is the information broadcast from the Android USB framework to the Android framework about the new USB headset's sound card details. So, if you can broadcast the USB_AUDIO_ DEVICE_PLUG intent with necessary sound card details, the Android device will play audio over the USB headset. In the following section, you learn how to send the USB_AUDIO_DEVICE_PLUG intent with the necessary sound card details to the Android audio framework.

The first step is put the Android device into USB host mode by connecting a USB headset. In the example setup, a Logitech USB handset was connected to the Android device and enumerated, as shown in Figure 6-5.

```
root@android:/ # lsusb
lsusb
Bus 001 Device 001: ID 1d6b:0002
Bus 001 Device 002: ID 04b4:6572
Bus 001 Device 003: ID 046d:0a14
```

Figure 6-5. Snapshot of USB enumeration detail in android

Note that this command for listing the connected USB devices works only if the device is rooted. If the device is not rooted, you can skip this step. Once the USB enumeration is successful, the next step is to confirm if a sound card is successfully created when the usb-core registers the USB audio device to the ALSA layer. This can be confirmed by reading the /proc/asound/cards file, as shown in Figure 6-6.

```
root@android:/dev/snd # cat /proc/asound/cards
cat /proc/asound/cards
 0 [omap4wm8994   ]: - omap4_wm8994
                      omap4_wm8994
 1 [OMAP4HDMI     ]: - OMAP4HDMI
                      OMAP4HDMI
 2 [Headset       ]: USB-Audio - Logitech USB Headset
                      Logitech Logitech USB Headset at usb-musb-hdrc-1.2, full speed
```

Figure 6-6. Snapshot of soundcard detail within android device

This confirms that the USB headset has been successfully registered with the ALSA layer and that a sound card has been created. It is time to send a broadcast to indicate a USB headset sound card to the Android audio framework. This can be achieved by using the am broadcast command, as shown in Figure 6-7.

```
root@android:/dev/snd # am broadcast -a android.intent.action.USB_AUDIO_DEVICE_PLUG --ei state 1 --ei card 2 --ei device 0
ent.action.USB_AUDIO_DEVICE_PLUG --ei state 1 --ei card 2 --ei device 0     <
Broadcasting: Intent { act=android.intent.action.USB_AUDIO_DEVICE_PLUG (has extras) }
Broadcast completed: result=0
```

Figure 6-7. Snapshot of intent broadcast detail

As described in the previous sections, the USB_AUDIO_DEVICE_PLUG intent has three parameters containing sound card details. As you saw in the previous step, the headset has the card number 2 and you can retrieve detailed information using the aplay -l command. A detailed description of the am broadcast command is available in its help, which will help interpret the previous broadcast. You can confirm successful execution from the terminal, which displays Broadcast completed: result=0. A simple analysis of the logs captured through logcat will confirm that the Android audio framework received the intent, as shown here:

```
D/dalvikvm( 1989): Note: class Landroid/app/ActivityManagerNative; has 165
unimplemented (abstract) methods
V/AudioService(  398): Broadcast Receiver: Got ACTION_USB_AUDIO_DEVICE_PLUG,
state = 1, card: 2, device: 0
I/AudioFlinger(  121): HAL output buffer size 1024 frames, normal mix buffer
size 1024 frames
```

Now the Android device is ready to stream data over the USB headset, which you can confirm by playing a song using a music player.

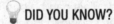 **DID YOU KNOW?**

The issue of not generating USB_AUDIO_DEVICE_PLUG has been reported in Google's bug repository and it confirms that Jelly Bean does not support USB audio devices other than the accessory support, as evidenced at https://code.google.com/p/android/issues/detail?id=36661.

USB Device Audio

The Jelly Bean Android CDD mandates that USB device audio functionality and Android-powered devices are expected to support audio traffic over the USB device mode as per the USB audio specification. The top-level requirement from Google is that an Android-powered device should support a standard USB audio class interface that is capable of two-channel, 16-bit PCM audio with a bit rate of 44.100kHz. This feature of an Android-powered device allows vendors to come up with audio accessories and end users to enjoy digital audio using an Android-powered device.

USB device audio functionality is similar to the USB host audio functionality in that the device just acts as a transport medium to send and receive audio streams in a timely manner. In a typical audio playback setup, a USB host streams data out and the USB audio device plays it. However, it is also possible to have an audio setup where the USB device streams data and the USB host plays it. Figure 6-8 illustrates an audio accessory mode in which the Android accessory hardware acts as a USB host.

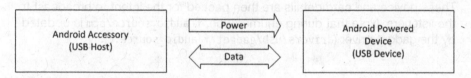

Figure 6-8. A simple Android accessory setup

After successfully configuring an Android-powered device in accessory mode for audio, data plays from the Android-powered device to the Android accessory. In the Jelly Bean version of Android, the USB audio device is supported only in output mode (IN transfers, device-to-host). There is much less information on audio device topology and audio control request support, other than what is already available on the kernel code.

Android-powered devices make the audio functionality available to end users in combination with an accessory or ADB class. In USB-specific terminology, an Android-powered device communicates its audio functionality in the descriptors sent to the USB host during enumeration. When the device switches to Android accessory mode, Google proposes that the audio functionality and the accessory class be specified in one of the following combinations. The hexadecimal numbers on the left represent the PID (Product ID) in the USB device descriptor when supporting the said functionality:

- 0x2D02 - Audio
- 0x2D03 - Audio and adb
- 0x2D04 - Accessory and audio
- 0x2D05 - Accessory, audio, and adb

We'll now explore the Android USB device audio framework and demonstrate the device audio feature with an example. To start with, we'll explore how the Android USB framework interfaces with the kernel USB gadget framework in accessory audio setup. Figure 6-9 illustrates a top-level architectural view of the Android audio accessory framework. As illustrated in Figure 6-9, the Android USB Service manager is responsible for indicating the availability of accessory sound cards to the Android audio framework. The USB Service Manager achieves this by listening to uevents generated by the gadget driver and subsequently reading the /sys/class/android_ usb/android0/f_audio_source/pcm file to collect card and device details. These device and card details are then packed for the intent to broadcast to the listeners. Note that during enumeration, f_audio_source/pcm is updated by the gadget driver (drivers/usb/gadget/f_audio_source.c).

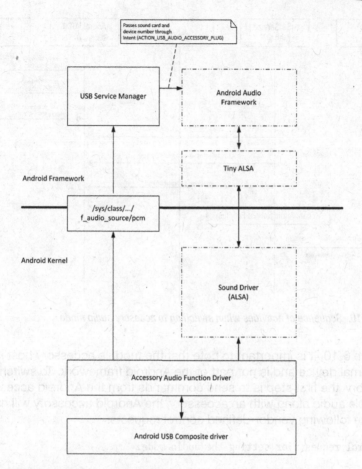

Figure 6-9. *Android USB device audio architecture*

Having read about the building blocks of the Android USB device audio, we'll now explore how to switch an Android-powered device to USB accessory mode with audio support.

Switching to Accessory Device Audio Mode

The Android accessory audio functionality, unlike other functionalities such as MTP, ADB, and mass storage, is not supported in the default configuration of an Android device. As explained earlier, the audio function is presented as one or more USB interfaces with the device functioning in accessory mode. This means an Android-powered device has to be put in accessory mode to enable the USB audio functionality. Figure 6-10 illustrates the sequence of activities that happens internally when an Android device switches to an accessory audio device.

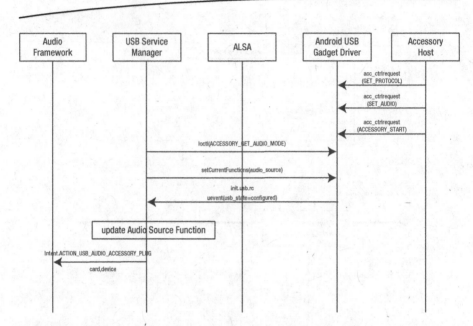

Figure 6-10. *Sequence of activities when switching to accesory audio mode*

In Figure 6-10, it is important to note that the module accessory host is an external device and is not part of the Android framework. To switch the accessory, the first step is to send commands from the Android accessory. To enable audio along with an accessory, the Android accessory will have to send the following vendor-defined control requests:

```
/* Control request for setting the audio mode.
 *
 * requestType:      USB_DIR_OUT | USB_TYPE_VENDOR
 * request:          ACCESSORY_SET_AUDIO_MODE
 * value:            0 - no audio
 *                   1 - device to host, 44100 16-bit stereo PCM
 * index:            0
 * data              none
 */
#define ACCESSORY_SET_AUDIO_MODE          58
```

Once these requests are successful, the Android accessory switches the Android-powered device to accessory mode, using the following request:

```
/* Control request for starting device in accessory mode.
 * The host sends this after setting all its strings to the device.
 *
 * requestType:      USB_DIR_OUT | USB_TYPE_VENDOR
 * request:          ACCESSORY_START
 * value:            0
```

```
*   index:          0
*   data            none
*/
#define ACCESSORY_START         53
```

When this request is received by the Android-powered device, the kernel driver indicates the Android USB Service framework to start accessory mode through uevent. The Android USB Service framework's UEvent observer then calls the startAccessoryMode function to set the accessory mode as the current USB functionality of the Android-powered device.

As you read in Chapter 2, current USB functionality of an Android device is managed by the user space framework through the sysfs interface, and is also applicable for use with this audio device case. The sysfs managing command exists in the /system/core/rootdir/init.usb.rc file, and the following snippet shows the device audio and adb configuration:

```
# USB and audio accessory configuration
on property:sys.usb.config=accessory,audio_source
    write /sys/class/android_usb/android0/enable 0
    write /sys/class/android_usb/android0/idVendor 18d1
    write /sys/class/android_usb/android0/idProduct 2d04
    write /sys/class/android_usb/android0/functions ${sys.usb.config}
    write /sys/class/android_usb/android0/enable 1
    setprop sys.usb.state ${sys.usb.config}
```

The Android USB gadget driver creates additional system file entries for each USB function that it supports, which are then used by user space modules. In the case of audio function, the Android USB gadget framework extends sound card details using the /sys/class/android_usb/android0/ f_audio_source/pcm file. This file is read for the details of the sound card and the intent is packed with card details to be broadcasted. This action is managed by the updateAudioSourceFunction function, and is called to state changes in the Android USB gadget driver, as indicated by USB_STATE uevents.

 DID YOU KNOW?

Inside the kernel, when the user space sets the USB functions, the USB gadget driver registers the sound driver of Linux (ALSA), and a PCM sound card audio_source is created, as shown. The following /proc entries are from an Android-powered device that lists the sound card details, similar to what was discussed in the USB host section.

```
root@android:/ # cat /proc/asound/cards
cat /proc/asound/cards
0 [omap4wm8994   ]: - omap4_wm8994
                     omap4_wm8994
1 [OMAP4HDMI     ]: - OMAP4HDMI
                     OMAP4HDMI
2 [audiosource   ]: audio_source - audio_source
                     USB accessory audio source
```

The Android audio service framework listens to this accessory audio broadcast in the frameworks/base/media/java/android/media/ AudioService.java file, as shown:

```
} else if (action.equals(Intent.ACTION_USB_AUDIO_ACCESSORY_PLUG) ||
           action.equals(Intent.ACTION_USB_AUDIO_DEVICE_PLUG)) {
   state = intent.getIntExtra("state", 0);
   int alsaCard = intent.getIntExtra("card", -1);
   int alsaDevice = intent.getIntExtra("device", -1);
   String params = (alsaCard == -1 && alsaDevice == -1 ? ""
                    : "card=" + alsaCard + ";device=" + alsaDevice);
   device = action.equals(Intent.ACTION_USB_AUDIO_ACCESSORY_PLUG) ?
           AudioSystem.DEVICE_OUT_USB_ACCESSORY : AudioSystem.
DEVICE_OUT_USB_DEVICE;
--cut---
   setWiredDeviceConnectionState(device, state, params);
```

The audio service framework extracts USB accessory sound card details. When you start playing music in a music player, the data is streamed over the USB interface. How the audio framework further manages the USB sound card is beyond the scope of the book.

Now that you've seen how an Android-powered device switches to audio mode, you can learn how to develop an audio-docking device that switches an Android device to accessory audio mode, receives the data, and then plays the audio with a real embedded setup.

Example: Android Accessory Audio Dock Using Cypress FX3

To develop an Android accessory, the first step is to identify a controller chip with USB host support that also provides an interface to audio devices. This example uses Cypress Semiconductor's EZ-USB FX3 development kit CYUSB3KIT and a DAC board, which supports I2S as input to play audio. Figure 6-11 illustrates typical blocks of an Android accessory audio dock.

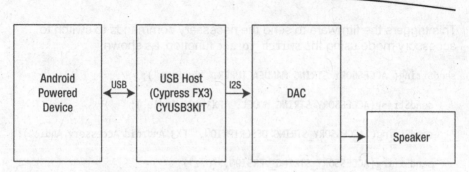

Figure 6-11. *The Android accessory audio dock setup*

ANDROID-POWERED DEVICE

This runs the Jelly Bean version of Android and streams audio over an ISO endpoint when in accessory audio mode.

USB HOST (CYPRESS FX3)

This controller runs Android accessory host firmware that enables the accessory mode in the Android device. It receives the audio data over the ISO endpoint and writes to a DAC over the I2S interface.

DAC (DIGITAL TO ANALOG CONVERTER)

The digital-to-analog converter (DAC) plays the digital data (the song) into the speaker.

Now that you have an understanding of the different blocks of the audio dock, let's explore the FX3 firmware code. To start the development, install the EZ-USB FX3 SDK, available from http://www.cypress.com/?rID=57990. Once the installation is successful, open the Android audio project called FX3_AOA_Audio from the CD.

Prepare the setup explained in the Figure 6-11 and program the firmware. Now connect the Android device to the FX3 controller board and it will bring the following firmware control to CyFxApplnStart in cyfxusbhost.c

This triggers the firmware to send the necessary commands to switch to accessory mode using the switch_to_acc function, as shown:

```
sendString( ACCESSORY_STRING_MANUFACTURER, "Cypress");

    sendString(ACCESSORY_STRING_MODEL, "FX3 AOA Audio");

    sendString( ACCESSORY_STRING_DESCRIPTION, "FX3 Android Accessory Audio");

    sendString(ACCESSORY_STRING_VERSION, "0.1");

    sendString(ACCESSORY_STRING_URI, "www.cypress.com");

    sendString(ACCESSORY_STRING_SERIAL, "0123456789");

    status = CyFxSendSetupRqt(
                USB_SETUP_HOST_TO_DEVICE |
                USB_SETUP_TYPE_VENDOR |
                USB_SETUP_RECIPIENT_DEVICE,
                SET_AUDIO_MODE, 1,0,
                0,0);

    status = CyFxSendSetupRqt(
                USB_SETUP_HOST_TO_DEVICE |
                USB_SETUP_TYPE_VENDOR |
                USB_SETUP_RECIPIENT_DEVICE,
                ACCESSORY_START, 0,0,
                0,0);
```

After the control commands are sent, the Android device re-enumerates in accessory mode, thereby exposing audio and accessory interfaces as discussed in previous sections.

Now get the audio interface details and claim an isochronous (ISO) endpoint to collect the audio data. Then pipe the audio data collected in the ISO to the I2S channel, as shown in this code:

```
/* Add the IN endpoint. */
  CyU3PMemSet ((uint8_t *)&epCfg, 0, sizeof(epCfg));
  epCfg.type = CY_U3P_USB_EP_ISO;
  epCfg.mult = 1;
  epCfg.maxPktSize = 256;
  epCfg.pollingRate = 1;
  /* Since DMA buffer sizes can only be multiple of 16 bytes and
   * also since this is an interrupt endpoint where the max data
   * packet size is same as the maxPktSize field, the fullPktSize
   * has to be a multiple of 16 bytes. */
  size = ((256 + 0x0F) & ~0x0F);
```

```
    epCfg.fullPktSize = size;
    epCfg.isStreamMode = CyTrue;
    status = CyU3PUsbHostEpAdd (0x83, &epCfg);
    if (status != CY_U3P_SUCCESS)
    {
        goto enum_error;
    }
    CyU3PDebugPrint (4, "EP Config success\r\n");

    /* Create a DMA channel for this EP. */
    CyU3PMemSet ((uint8_t *)&dmaCfg, 0, sizeof(dmaCfg));
    dmaCfg.size = size;
    dmaCfg.count = 6;
    dmaCfg.prodSckId = (CyU3PDmaSocketId_t)(CY_U3P_UIB_SOCKET_PROD_0 + (0x0F
& 0x83));
    dmaCfg.consSckId = CY_U3P_CPU_SOCKET_CONS;
    dmaCfg.dmaMode = CY_U3P_DMA_MODE_BYTE;
    dmaCfg.notification = CY_U3P_DMA_CB_PROD_EVENT;
    dmaCfg.cb = CyFxAoADmaCb;
    dmaCfg.prodHeader = 0;
    dmaCfg.prodFooter = 0;
    dmaCfg.consHeader = 0;
    dmaCfg.prodAvailCount = 0;
    status = CyU3PDmaChannelCreate (&glHostAoACh, CY_U3P_DMA_TYPE_MANUAL_IN,
&dmaCfg);
    if (status != CY_U3P_SUCCESS)
    {
        goto app_error;
    }

    dmaCfg.prodSckId = CY_U3P_CPU_SOCKET_PROD;
    dmaCfg.consSckId = CY_U3P_LPP_SOCKET_I2S_LEFT;
    dmaCfg.notification = 0;
    dmaCfg.cb = NULL;
    status = CyU3PDmaChannelCreate (&glI2SLeftCh, CY_U3P_DMA_TYPE_MANUAL_OUT,
&dmaCfg);
    if (status != CY_U3P_SUCCESS)
    {
    goto app_error;
    }

    dmaCfg.prodSckId = CY_U3P_CPU_SOCKET_PROD;
    dmaCfg.consSckId = CY_U3P_LPP_SOCKET_I2S_RIGHT;
    status = CyU3PDmaChannelCreate (&glI2SRightCh, CY_U3P_DMA_TYPE_MANUAL_
OUT, &dmaCfg);
    if (status != CY_U3P_SUCCESS)
    {
        goto app_error;
    }
```

```
CyU3PDebugPrint (4, "DMA Config success\r\n");

status = CyU3PDmaChannelSetXfer (&glI2SLeftCh, 0);
if (status != CY_U3P_SUCCESS)
{
    goto app_error;
}
CyU3PDebugPrint (4, "left out success\r\n");

status = CyU3PDmaChannelSetXfer (&glI2SRightCh, 0);
if (status != CY_U3P_SUCCESS)
{
 CyU3PDebugPrint (4, "right out failed 0x%x\r\n", status);
    goto app_error;
}
CyU3PDebugPrint (4, "right out success\r\n");

/* Enable EP transfer. In stream mode, the transfer size should be zero.
*/
    status = CyU3PUsbHostEpSetXfer (0x83, CY_U3P_USB_HOST_EPXFER_NORMAL,
0);
if (status != CY_U3P_SUCCESS)
{
    goto app_error;
  }
  CyU3PDebugPrint (4, "hostepsetxfer success\r\n");

/* Set for infinite transfer. */
status = CyU3PDmaChannelSetXfer (&glHostAoACh, 0);
if (status != CY_U3P_SUCCESS)
{
    goto app_error;
}
```

Now open a media player in the Android device and play an audio file. This streams audio to the FX3 host, which subsequently pipes it to the DAC board over the I2S channel. Figure 6-12 captures the audio data over the ISO endpoint using a bus analyzer.

⊞ ← IN transaction	1	3		HS	176 bytes (5E FE 59 04 C6 FE 98 0...	31.635 01...
⊞ ← IN transaction	1	3		HS	176 bytes (05 0B C1 FB 53 0A F1 F...	31.635 14...
⊞ ← IN transaction	1	3		HS	176 bytes (F4 F3 DF FF 03 F4 CC F...	31.635 26...
⊞ ✕ Incomplete IN transaction	1	3	...	HS	No data	31.635 39...
⊞ ← IN transaction	1	3		HS	176 bytes (CE 07 E9 FD EF 07 23 F...	31.635 51...
⊞ ← IN transaction	1·	3		HS	176 bytes (C5 03 A8 05 BC 03 FC ...	31.635 64...
⊞ ← IN transaction	1	3		HS	176 bytes (67 FC BC F7 86 FC 23 ...	31.635 76...
⊞ ✕ Incomplete IN transaction	1	3	...	HS	No data	31.635 89...
⊞ ← IN transaction	1	3		HS	176 bytes (98 FD 0A FD 7C FD 15 ...	31.636 01...
⊞ ← IN transaction	1	3		HS	176 bytes (42 FE 99 FF 36 FF 7C F...	31.636 14...
⊞ ← IN transaction	1	3		HS	176 bytes (40 0A 5E 04 B2 09 39 0...	31.636 26...
⊞ ← IN transaction	1	3		HS	176 bytes (4E FB 28 FA 37 FB 0A F...	31.636 39...
⊞ ← IN transaction	1	3		HS	176 bytes (52 03 2A 00 07 03 3C 0...	31.636 51...
⊞ ← IN transaction	1	3		HS	176 bytes (D8 FC C7 01 5B FC 9B ...	31.636 64...
⊞ ✕ Incomplete IN transaction	1	3	...	HS	No data	31.636 76...
⊞ ← IN transaction	1	3		HS	176 bytes (C6 03 31 02 8F 04 79 0...	31.636 89...
⊞ ← IN transaction	1	3		HS ·	176 bytes (BC FD 1D F9 11 FE 61 ...	31.637 01...
⊞ ← IN transaction	1	3		HS	176 bytes (DF 00 2F 00 8D 01 04 0...	31.637 14...
⊞ ✕ Incomplete IN transaction	1	3	...	HS	No data	31.637 26...
⊞ ← IN transaction	1	3		HS	176 bytes (26 00 0F 04 FF FF 27 04...	31.637 39...
⊞ ← IN transaction	1	3		HS	176 bytes (B2 00 98 00 DA 00 10 0...	31.637 51...
⊞ ← IN transaction	1	3		HS	176 bytes (BA F5 DB FA BA F5 6C...	31.637 64...
⊞ ✕ Incomplete IN transaction	1	3	...	HS	No data	31.637 76...
⊞ ← IN transaction	1	3		HS	176 bytes (88 FC 2D FF B1 FC 2E ...	31.637 89...
⊞ ← IN transaction	1	3		HS	176 bytes (F5 03 33 0A 59 03 C1 0...	31.638 01...
⊞ ← IN transaction	1	3		HS	176 bytes (0E FF 5B 05 AC FE 03 0...	31.638 14...
⊞ ← IN transaction	1	3		HS	176 bytes (57 F9 94 FB 31 F9 D1 F...	31.638 26...
⊞ ← IN transaction	1	3		HS	176 bytes (09 FE 88 FF 32 FE C9 F...	31.638 39...
⊞ ← IN transaction	1	3		HS	176 bytes (DA 0C 09 05 C0 0C 28 ...	31.638 51...

Figure 6-12. The ISO transfers when audio is played

Conclusion

Multimedia is one of the key functionalities in any mobile device and is used as a key selling point. Among other multimedia features, audio is an important feature that makes all the difference and convinces users to buy a mobile device. Models like the "Walkman" series by many mobile manufacturers are proof of this. To cater to this market and enhance user experience, the Android Jelly Bean version introduced USB device audio features. This chapter detailed this device audio framework, along with examples of the USB host audio.

An important reason why Google included accessory device audio features was to allow manufacturers to come up with new accessories for Android-powered devices. Though there are numerous audio accessories available in the market, the important difference is that they do not comply with USB specifications and are referred to as analog audio accessories.

## Chapter 7

Android Debug Bridge (ADB)

What You Will Learn:

- ADB Overview
- Setting Up ADB
- ADB Protocol
- ADB Framework Architecture
- Exercises: Debugging Using JDB and Backup Using ADB

Android Debug Bridge, popularly referred to as ADB, is the tool that Google provides along with the Android framework to facilitate debugging and managing an Android system. ADB uses USB or TCP as its transport layer to communicate with an Android-powered device. ADB works in a simple client/server architecture, and is made up of three key components, namely:

A **server** runs in the background of the host system and communicates between the client and the ADB daemon running on an emulator or device. The server also maintains details of the connected device along with its state.

A **client** on the host system that connects to the server, which can be an adb shell or adb logcat command that runs on a terminal to the Dalvik Debug Monitor Server (DDMS) tool.

An ADB **daemon** that runs on the Android device/emulator as part of the Android USB framework and interacts with the server to help manage the Android-powered device.

It is important to note that on a host environment, the ADB server and the ADB client share the same binary in the host environment. Figure 7-1 illustrates how these three components fit in an ADB setup.

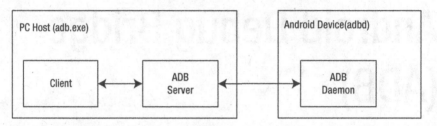

Figure 7-1. An ADB setup with its three key modules

This section discusses how these modules fit in a real setup with a couple of examples. One of the most commonly used ADB commands is the adb shell command. Assume that an Android device is connected to the host PC using a USB with the Android Debug Bridge option enabled on the device by going to Settings ➤ Developer Options. In this scenario, the terminal where the ABD shell is running is the client, and the command invokes the ADB server adb on the host PC. The ADB server then talks to the host PC to the ADB daemon adbd on the Android device over the USB to service the shell commands.

Another example is the Dalvik Debug Monitor Server (DDMS) debugging tool, an eclipse plug-in tool that provides screen captures and logcat, and processes information for an Android device. The DDMS tool in the background relies on ADB's services for its operations. In this setup, the DDMS tool is the client component of the ADB setup. Figure 7-2 illustrates the terminal and DDMS of an ADB setup.

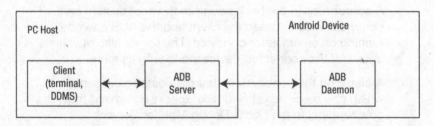

Figure 7-2. A terminal/DDMS ADB setup

Having briefly explored the building blocks of an ADB setup and how it internally communicates, the following sections explore how to set up ADB on a PC host, the protocol used by ADB to communicate, and its architecture and features list. Finally, the chapter includes an example of how to use JDB with ADB and back up with ADB.

Setting Up ADB

To set up ADB on a host PC, the first step is to download the Android SDK from the following link: http://developer.android.com/sdk/index.html. The following section explores how to set up ADB in Windows and Linux.

Windows

When extracting the SDK, you can find the adb.exe tool in the adt-bundle-windows-x86-20130917\sdk\platform-tools folder. Since the SDK package does not update the PATH, you have to set the platform tools folder in the PATH environmental variable. This will allow you to run ADB from any location from a command prompt.

Now, connect an Android-powered device to the host PC with ADB enabled under Developer options. This should make the ADB function available to the host PC, and can be confirmed using a simple ADB command called adb devices. This command will print a list of all attached emulator/device instances. Sometimes, you may need to configure a USB vendor ID for the Android-powered device in a special file called adb_usb.ini.

This file will be created in the .android folder in the user's home directory ($HOME) when installing the ADB setup. (For example, c:/Users/<user name>/.android for Windows7). If the folder has not been created yet, this folder has to be created along with the adb_usb.ini file. This setup is required because internally within the ABD host implementation, vendor IDs are matched (is_adb_interface) against a set of built-in vendor IDs, which are defined in system/core/adb/usb_vendors.c#builtInVendorIds. The ADB host implementation reads the INI file in order to update the vendor ID list, along with the existing built-in vendor ID list in system/core/adb/usb_vendors.c (the usb_vendors_init function).

You can also set the ANDROID_SDK_HOME environmental variable if for some reason you want to place the .android folder in a different location. This environmental variable should be set to the path of the .android folder, which is read by the ADB implementation for the INI file path.

Linux

In Linux, the same rules apply, except in regard to how these rules are actually set. To enable ADB to be run from any location from a terminal, set the PATH environmental variable with the installation path.

```
export PATH=${PATH}:/<>/android-sdk-linux/tools
export PATH=${PATH}:/<>/android-sdk-linux/platform-tools
```

The .android/adb_usb.ini folder can be created in the user's home folder to add any unsupported vendor IDs, just like with the Windows setup. The only difference in a Linux setup is that you have to provide permission for a normal user account to be able to access the ADB interface of the USB device. This can be achieved by adding udev rules, as discussed below, with execution permission in the /etc/udev/rules.d/androids.rules file.

```
$ cat /etc/udev/rules.d/androids.rules
SUBSYSTEM=="usb", ATTR{idVendor}=="04B4", MODE="0666"
```

Now, when you run the adb devices command on the terminal, the Android device will be listed with a serial number.

If the ADB is not be detected evenafter going through the above mentioned steps, then In this situation, you might have to restart the ADB server by running the adb kill-server command.

 DID YOU KNOW?

As of Android 4.2, the ADB tool was made more secure. The Developer Option menu option, which allows you to enable ADB, is hidden. To enable this option, you have to tap Build Number seven times from the Settings ➤ About Phone option.

ADB Protocol

Recall that there are two types of ADB commands. There are ADB commands whose information lies within the server, and there are ADB commands that require fetching information from the daemon on the Android-powered device by the ADB server. A command that is serviced within the server without communicating with the Android device is referred to as *host service,* and commands that are serviced after fetching information from the device through the daemon are termed *local services*. In this section, we'll explore the protocol involved in the host service and the local service, which is over a transport medium like USB.

Client <-> Server Protocol

In an ADB setup, the mode of communication between a client and a server is through standard socket programming over TCP. In this setup, the ADB server listens to TCP port 5037 of the host, to which the client has to send the request. The format of the request that the client has to send is shown in Figure 7-3.

4 byte length	Payload	
	host:	<command>
	host-serial:	<command>
	shell:	<command>

Figure 7-3. The protocol packet format

The request from an ADB client should contain an initial four-byte field in ASCII and a payload. The payload generally starts with the prefix keyword host:, which indicates that the request is addressed to the server. Upon receiving the request, the server will reply with an OKAY or FAIL string to indicate the status of the request. That string is then followed by an optional payload containing the length and requested data. To better understand practically how the packets are seen on the socket, you can use a TCP port-monitoring tool like Wireshark or tcpdump. Figure 7-4 shows how a client's request will look with various ADB commands.

```
19 0.000513 127.0.0.1 127.0.0.1 TCP      66 5037 > 50678 [ACK] Seq=1 Ack=17 Win=43776 Len=0 TSval=407188557 TSecr=407188557
20 0.000553 127.0.0.1 127.0.0.1 TCP      98 5037 > 50678 [PSH, ACK] Seq=1 Ack=17 Win=43776 Len=32 TSval=407188557 TSecr=407188557
21 0.000574 127.0.0.1 127.0.0.1 TCP      66 5037 > 50678 [FIN, ACK] Seq=33 Ack=17 Win=43776 Len=0 TSval=407188557 TSecr=407188557
22 0.000575 127.0.0.1 127.0.0.1 TCP      66 50678 > 5037 [ACK] Seq=17 Ack=33 Win=43776 Len=0 TSval=407188557 TSecr=407188557
23 0.000608 127.0.0.1 127.0.0.1 TCP      66 50678 > 5037 [FIN, ACK] Seq=17 Ack=34 Win=43776 Len=0 TSval=407188557 TSecr=407188557
24 0.000620 127.0.0.1 127.0.0.1 TCP      66 5037 > 50678 [ACK] Seq=34 Ack=18 Win=43776 Len=0 TSval=407188557 TSecr=407188557

▶ Frame 20: 98 bytes on wire (784 bits), 98 bytes captured (784 bits)
▶ Ethernet II, Src: 00:00:00_00:00:00 (00:00:00:00:00:00), Dst: 00:00:00_00:00:00 (00:00:00:00:00:00)
▶ Internet Protocol Version 4, Src: 127.0.0.1 (127.0.0.1), Dst: 127.0.0.1 (127.0.0.1)
▶ Transmission Control Protocol, Src Port: 5037 (5037), Dst Port: 50678 (50678), Seq: 1, Ack: 17, Len: 32
▶ Data (32 bytes)
0000  00 00 00 00 00 00 00 00  00 00 00 00 08 00 45 00   .............E.
0010  00 54 36 e0 40 00 40 06  05 c2 7f 00 00 01 7f 00   .T6.@.@.........
0020  00 01 13 ad c5 f6 cf 87  02 93 2b e5 97 48 80 18   .........+..H.
0030  01 56 fe 48 00 00 01 01  08 0a 18 45 34 4d 18 45   .V.H....E4M.E
0040  34 4d 4f 4b 41 59 30 30  31 38 34 31 30 30 63 35   4MOKAY00 184100c5
0050  31 30 30 34 35 66 32 31  30 30 09 64 65 76 69 63   10045f21 00.devic
0060  65 0a                                              e.
```

Figure 7-4. Wireshark dump showing client and server communication over TCP

Server <-> ADB Daemon Protocol

There are command requests from ABD clients that require information from the Android-powered device or emulator. The ADB server uses two types of transport, mostly depending on the type of setup. When a host is connected to a physical Android-powered device over USB, it uses USB as the transport, and in the case of an Android emulator, the transport is through TCP. The protocol is simple and straightforward; it simply has to forward the packet to and from the server. The command messages of the protocol layer consist of a 24-byte header followed by an optional payload, (each field size is four bytes), as shown here:

```
struct message {
    unsigned command;        /* command identifier constant    */
    unsigned arg0;           /* first argument                 */
    unsigned arg1;           /* second argument                */
    unsigned data_length;    /* length of payload (0 is allowed) */
    unsigned data_crc32;     /* crc32 of data payload          */
    unsigned magic;          /* command ^ 0xffffffff           */
};
```

The message can contain any of the following commands with the data length, which indicates the payload length, and are generally quoted as a string of ASCII characters.

```
#define A_SYNC 0x434e5953
#define A_CNXN 0x4e584e43
#define A_AUTH 0x48545541
#define A_OPEN 0x4e45504f
#define A_OKAY 0x59414b4f
#define A_CLSE 0x45534c43
#define A_WRTE 0x45545257
```

You can read more detailed information on the format of the command and services of the two protocols in the following files:

- system/core/adb/SERVICES.TXT

- system/core/adb/OVERVIEW.TXT

- system/core/adb/protocol.txt

After you gain an understanding of ADB protocols and their setup, the following section explores how this protocol is implemented in a host and an Android device environment. This section also covers activity sequences on how the information flows to and from the Android daemon in the Android USB framework.

To understand the sequence of activities in a typical ADB setup, consider two simple ADB commands, namely adb devices and adb shell ls, which will cover the two kinds of services an ADB client can encounter. Before using any of these services, the ADB protocol starts with the connect command, which establishes the presence of the remote system. Both the host ADB and the ADB daemon send a connect message when the connection is established. The connect command is attached with a payload that provides version, system identification, string, and the maximum data that the ADB connection can hold. Once this state is achieved, the ADB setup is ready for communication. Any command message sent before this command is ignored.

Once the connection is established, a user can execute ADB commands. Figure 7-5 illustrates the flow of information when the adb devices and adb shell ls commands are executed. When the adb devices command is executed, you will notice that the ADB server responds to the command locally, without contacting the ADB daemon. The ADB server maintains information on the list of connected devices and their state, which it uses to respond to certain ADB commands, generally termed as "host services."

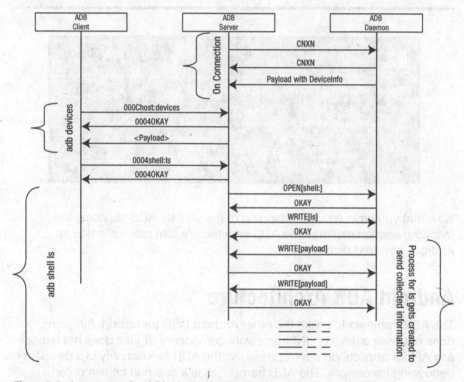

Figure 7-5. A sequence of activities between the client, the server, and the daemon

In the next command setup, the command is served by the ADB daemon, and the ADB server facilitates the command by initiating, and subsequently acting in, the pass-through mode. This command generally starts a service within the ADB daemon or on the device the client interacts with. Figure 7-5 displays sequential activity for a non-interactive command. As an example, the adb shell ls command is illustrated.

DID YOU KNOW?

An ADB connection had to be authenticated for ADB to work from Android version 4.2.2. If an authentication process is not completed before executing the adb devices command, the device will be listed as offline. Also, if you use just any old SDK setup, it will not work, and you will have to download the latest SDK. ADB authentication is done with an RSA key pair. ADB daemon on a device can maintain a list of hosts (PCs) that have been authenticated so that they need not be authenticated each time. (Always allow the "This Computer" option to be enabled, as shown in the figure.)

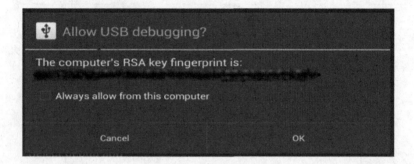

Now that you have an understanding of the various ADB services, the following section explores the ADB architecture that resides inside an Android-powered device.

Android ADB Architecture

The ADB framework, unlike the other Android USB framework functions, does not have a Java or JNI framework component. It also does not expose any API for application development, as the ADB functionality is a developer debugging framework. The ADB framework is a daemon implemented in the C language running in the Android user space. This daemon is facilitated by the Android USB framework, namely UsbDeviceManager and UsbDebuggingManager. Figure 7-6 provides the building blocks of ADB framework within an Android powered device.

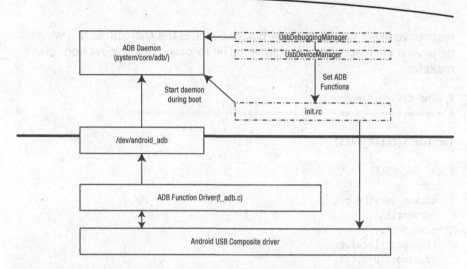

Figure 7-6. The building blocks of ADB inside an Android-powered device

The UsbDeviceManager in the ADB use case is used to enable and disable ADB functionality, as detailed in Chapter 2. The UsbDebuggingManager was introduced with the Jelly Bean 4.2 version of Android, when the RSA-based authentication feature was added for ADB. The UsbDebuggingManager. java implementation can be found in the following directory along with the UsbService framework: frameworks/base/services/java/com/android/ server/usb/. The UsbDebuggingManager opens a line to communicate with an ADB daemon and acts as an interface between the user feedback on authentication and the ADB daemon.

It can be inferred from Figure 7-6 that the ADB daemon implementation relies on the Android kernel USB driver framework to send and receive messages to an ADB server. The ADB daemon, which is a process that starts when the device boots up, is generally started from the init.rc script. The ADB implementation can be located in the /system/core/adb folder of the Android framework. This folder contains the implementation of both the ADB daemon and the ADB application that runs on a host. These two applications share common files with code that is separated by the ADB_HOST macro, including adb.c, transport.c, and transport_local.c.

You might also remember that the ADB executables share the same binary on a host environment with the ADB client implementation. The ADB client implementation is implemented through the key files called commandline.c and adb_client.c. The source files in the system/core/adb are for the ADB server and the ADB daemon. To determine the exact files that implement respective executables, the best place to look is the Android.mk file, which generates the respective executables. The following is a snippet from the makefile:

```
# adbd device daemon
# =============================================================

include $(CLEAR_VARS)

LOCAL_SRC_FILES := \
    adb.c \
    backup_service.c \
    fdevent.c \
    transport.c \
    transport_local.c \
    transport_usb.c \
    adb_auth_client.c \
    sockets.c \
    services.c \
    file_sync_service.c \
    jdwp_service.c \
    framebuffer_service.c \
    remount_service.c \
    usb_linux_client.c \
    log_service.c \
    utils.c

# adb host tool
# =================================================

LOCAL_SRC_FILES := \
    adb.c \
    console.c \
    transport.c \
    transport_local.c \
    transport_usb.c \
    commandline.c \
    adb_client.c \
    adb_auth_host.c \
    sockets.c \
    services.c \
    file_sync_client.c \
    $(EXTRA_SRCS) \
    $(USB_SRCS) \
    utils.c \
    usb_vendors.c
```

As you can infer from the file list, the ADB daemon and the host executable (adb.exe) share common files, and there are files that are specific to both implementations. As discussed, the common files separate the respective implementation by the ADB_HOST macro. The following section explores some of the key features of ADB and their usage.

Example 1: Using JDB with ADB

Android ADB integrates support for Java Debug Wire Protocol (JDWP), a protocol used for communication between a debugger and the virtual machine. This section provides a brief summary of the JDWP implementation and explains how to use Java Debugger (JDB) with ADB. It all starts with an ADB daemon starting a named Unix server socket called @vm-debug-control, which a JDWP thread connects to when it starts. After a successful connection, the JDWP threads the PID of the process as a string of four hexadecimal characters.

To connect a debugger, you can simply run the adb forward tcp:<hostport> jdwp:<pid> command with an interested PID. This indicates the ADB daemon to share the socket descriptor with the JDWP process. The JDWP process uses the descriptor as it passes through the connection to the debugger. The ADB JDWP implementation is spread across dalvik/vm/jdwp/JdwpAdb.cpp and system/core/adb/jdwp_service.c for detailed study.

Next you'll see how to get the list of PIDs that use a JDWP service, and then explore how to connect to the debugger JDB. The first step is to use the adb jdwp command, which lists the PIDs that implement JDWP, as shown here:

```
root@rajaram-pc:/home/rajaram#
root@rajaram-pc:/home/rajaram# adb jdwp
491
1384
1400
801
612
```

Now connect JDB to the JDWP process using the adb forward command, as shown in the following snippet. Then you connect to JDB using jdb -attach localhost:port.

```
root@rajaram-pc:/home/rajaram# adb forward tcp:8000 jdwp:1384
root@rajaram-pc:/home/rajaram# jdb -attach localhost:8000
Set uncaught java.lang.Throwable
Set deferred uncaught java.lang.Throwable
Initializing jdb ...
```

```
> threads
Group system:
  (java.lang.Thread)0xc141b1e358 <8> FinalizerWatchdogDaemon
cond. waiting
  (java.lang.Thread)0xc141b1e1a8 <7> FinalizerDaem          cond. waiting
```

Once you're connected with JDB, you can debug your application using the JDB commands.

Example 2: Backing Up Your Phone with ADB

Another key feature of ADB is the ability to back up your Android device to a host PC and then restore it on the device. This feature can be handy if you lose data from your Android device. The following command-line snippet lists the various adb backup options:

```
adb backup [-f <file>] [-apk|-noapk] [-shared|-noshared] [-all] [-system|-
nosystem] [<packages...>]
             - write an archive of the device's data to <file>.
         If no -f option is supplied then the data is written
         to "backup.ab" in the current directory.
         (-apk|-noapk enable/disable backup of the .apks themselves
             in the archive; the default is noapk.)
         (-shared|-noshared enable/disable backup of the device's
             shared storage / SD card contents; the default is noshared.)
         (-all means to back up all installed applications)
         (-system|-nosystem toggles whether -all automatically includes
             system applications; the default is to include system apps)
         (<packages...>is the list of applications to be backed up.  If
             the -all or -shared flags are passed, then the package
             list is optional.  Applications explicitly given on the
             command line will be included even if -nosystem would
             ordinarily cause them to be omitted.)
```

The backup command provides an option to choose the type of data for backup or even ignore certain data. This backup mechanism requires user intervention on the Android device side, as it provides the user an option to set a password for the backup and allow or deny the backup process, as shown in Figure 7-7.

Figure 7-7. *User interface option in an Android device when the ABD backup command is executed*

Battery Charging Using USB

What you will learn:

- Types of USB Chargers
- Overview of USB Battery Charging Specification
- Android USB Charging Framework
- Sample Application

USB technology has evolved over the years as the standard for connecting peripherals like keyboards, printers, and so on, to personal computers, and as a result, USB has replaced serial and parallel ports. Modern devices like smart phones and game controllers have also adopted this technology as a primary transport mechanism. As part of their evolution, USB evolved from a data interface to an important source of power to charge portable devices like a smart phones, or even to power up an external audio speaker. In *Battery Charging Specification*, the Battery Charging Working Group of the USB Implementers Forum (USB-IF) has standardized how a USB power source has to behave, the different types of USB power sources, and how much power a device can consume when connected to a USB source.

This appendix explores USB-based charging that you, as an Android developer, need to know to develop applications related to charging. This chapter initially explores the different types of USB chargers available, and explains how they are different, followed by exploring the USB specification that defines USB battery charging. Furthermore, this chapter will provide a quick overview of how Android framework implements battery charging functionality. It is important to note that this Android Battery Charging framework is not part of Android USB framework, as charging doesn't use conventional USB communication protocols. That's the reason this is an appendix to the book. At the end, this appendix also uses an example to explain how you can get additional information on a battery's condition, beyond just the battery charging status and the charge amount left.

Types of USB Chargers

As a typical user, you likely have multiple USB sources with which you can charge batteries or use for powering a device and consuming power. This section captures these different power sources in layman terms. Details of its characteristics are explained in the next section of USB battery specification overview.

Wall Charger

A typical USB charger that you receive along with a portable device is shown in Figure A-1.

Figure A-1. Illustration of a wall charger unit

In this setup, the power source for the charging device is an AC power point. The USB provides a medium of transferring power from the source to the portable device.

Personal Computer

When you have a host PC, say a desktop or a laptop computer, you can connect your portable device (or peripheral) to any of the PC's USB ports to charge it. In this case, the power source is the host PC, as shown in Figure A-2.

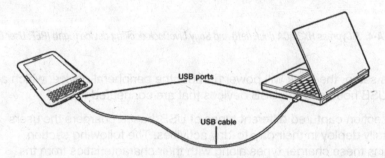

Figure A-2. A peripheral charging from a USB port of a PC (REF: Kindle documentation)

A USB car kit charger is also similar to this setup, where the power is sourced from the car's battery via a USB port.

Charging Dock

Another method for charging a portable device is through a charging dock. Such docking devices provide a couple of functions aside from just charging. The first example, shown in Figure A-3, is the Sony DK300. It can act as a docking station that supports charging the mobile device, along with a provision to play back audio as well.

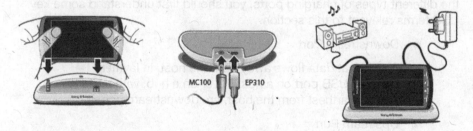

Figure A-3. Illustration of the audio docking station of Sony DK300 (REF: User Guide)

In today's market, you can find charging docks that provide functionalities like serving as a hub and ones that allow you to connect USB devices, both of which are shown in Figure A-4.

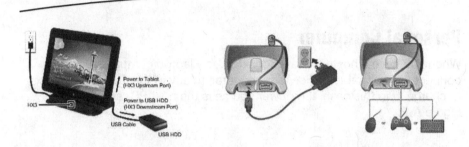

Figure A-4. A Cypress HX3 ACA dock (left) and Sony LiveDock docking device (right) (REF: User Guide)

In this setup, the dock will power up both the peripheral device, which acts as a USB host, and the USB devices that are connected to it.

This section captured different types of USB-based chargers the users generally deploy in their day-to-day activities. The following section explains these charger types along with their characteristics from the "Battery Charging 1.2" specification.

USB Battery Specification Overview

Having looked at different types of USB chargers in layman terms, you'll now read a quick overview of the Battery Charging 1.2 specification to understand the characteristics of these chargers in engineering terms.

In a way, the main focus of the battery specification is to define the characteristics of different chargers and describe their mechanisms for how to detect the chargers. This section focuses on the different types of charging options (USB ports and chargers) and their characteristics in brief. The specification also details the mechanism that can differentiate the different types, but that is beyond the scope of this book. Before you study the different types of charging ports, you should first understand some key USB terms relevant to this section.

- Downstream Port

    A port that data flows away from the host. In laymen terms, a USB port on a host PC or on a hub, with ports that are farthest from the host, are downstream ports.

- Upstream Port

    A port that sends data toward the host. Generally, a port on a USB device and on a hub, with the port that is closest to the host, are upstream ports.

Here are the different types of charging options (USB ports and chargers) and their characteristics:

■ Standard Downstream Port (SDP)

Refers to a port on a host or hub that's compliant with USB 2.0 specifications. This means a SDP port can provide different power, depending upon the state of connection with the USB device. An SDP port expects a downstream device to have the following maximum current consumption in different states:

■ 2.5mA when the device is in a suspended state

■ 100mA when connected and not configured

■ 500mA or the amount of current requested by the device's configuration descriptor, whichever is less, when configured

When a USB device is connected to a SDP, the device can draw 100mA and up to 500mA once the device is enumerated successfully by the host. The charging setup as described for the personal computer example of the previous section represents a Standard Downstream Port.

■ Charging Downstream Port (CDP))

Refers to a port on a host or hub that's compliant with USB 2.0 specifications. But unlike the SDP, a CDP port allows a USB device to draw more current, thereby facilitating faster charging. When a portable device is connected to a charging port, it is expected to behave in the following way:

■ 2.5mA when the device is in a suspended state

■ 100mA when it is connected and not configured

■ Maximum of 1.5A when configured

When a USB device is connected to a CDP, the device will be enumerated successfully by the host. The charging setup as described for the personal computer example of the previous section can also represent a Charging Downstream Port. A CDP port is generally marked with a symbol to indicate to the user that it can supply more power.

- Dedicated Charging Port (DCP)

  A downstream port that provides power over a USB connection to a portable device. When a portable device is connected to a DCP, a maximum of 1.5A can be consumed by the device. The key difference between a DCP and the other two charging ports is that the D+ and the D- lines are shorted, which means there is no support for enumeration. The wall charger example in the previous section is an example of a DCP.

- Accessory Charger Adapter (ACA)

  With portable devices becoming smaller to be more attractive and convenient to users, the number of ports available to the user becomes limited. On any given PD, you will generally find a single USB port in which you can connect a charger to charge the device or connect a USB device like a mouse or keyboard. Herein lies the problem of how to use a USB port for connecting a USB keyboard when the device requires charging.

  Accessory Charging Adapter (ACA) is aimed at addressing this problem by expanding a single USB port to be attached to a charger and a USB device at the same time, as shown in Figure A-5.

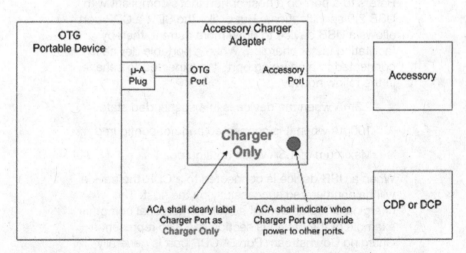

Figure A-5. ACA representation by battery charging specification (REF: USB Battery Charging Specification)

The dock examples discussed in the first section of this appendix belong to this class of device, and it supports the following three ports:

■ OTG port: This port allows users to dock the device with a Micro AB receptacle.

■ Accessory port: This port allows users to connect any device to the PD.

■ Charger port: This port allows users to connect a charger that can power up the PD and the accessory device.

An ACA is classified into two types, based on the features it supports. If an accessory port of an ACA has a Mirco-AB receptacle, allowing connection of A and B devices, it is referred to as Micro ACA. When the accessory port has only a Standard-A receptacle, which allows connection of a B device, the ACA device is referred to as a Standard ACA. Figure A-5 shows is a typical standard ACA setup.

 DID YOU KNOW?

Have you ever wondered why your portable device takes more time to charge when it's connected to a USB port of a host PC than when connected to a wall charger? The answer lies in the amount of current that is allowed to be consumed by a device from these ports. A Standard Downstream USB 2.0 Port in a host PC allows a maximum of 500mA of current to charge, whereas a wall charger (or a Charging Downstream Port on a host or hub) can provide more than 1 amp, thus enabling the wall unit to charge faster.

The battery-charging specification also talks about handling dead batteries, along with mechanisms to differentiate charging ports, and you can refer to the specification for more details. It's available at: http://www.usb.org/developers/devclass_docs/USB_Battery_Charging_1.2.pdf.

Android Battery Charging Overview

Android's USB battery charging requirement is very straightforward. According to Android CDD 4.2, the Android platform's USB charging requirement is as follows:

> *"It SHOULD implement support for USB battery charging specification. Existing and new devices that run Android 4.2 are very strongly encouraged to meet these requirements in Android 4.2 so they will be able to upgrade to the future platform releases."*

A device that claims to be compatible with Android CDD 4.2 supports all modes of USB charging, as explained in the previous section. Inside the Android platform, most of the charging-related activities like detecting the charger type and managing the battery, are done by the hardware and the Android Linux kernel. The Android kernel shares information related to battery charging using system file entries in the user space. The user space Android framework presents the user details of the hardware and kernel changes related to charging by reading the information exported by the kernel. This is managed by the following two blocks of the Android Battery framework.

Battery ManagerThis framework is implemented through the `frameworks/base/core/java/android/os/BatteryManager.java` file and acts as an interface between an application and the Battery Service framework. The `BatteryManager` class defines the constants for applications to extract information from the `ACTION_BATTERY_CHANGED` intent, which is generated by the Battery Service.

Battery Service

The Battery Service framework is the core part of the Android Battery framework. The Battery Service framework is responsible for generating battery state-related intents and broadcasting them to other Android frameworks. Internally, the battery service is divided into a class and a JNI implementation. The battery service java class is implemented in `frameworks/base/services/java/com/android/server/BatteryService.java` and the JNI part is implemented through `frameworks/base/services/jni/com_android_server_BatteryService.cpp`. The role of the JNI part is to read appropriate battery driver-related files exported by the Android kernel and pass them to the java class over global variables. The java class in turn interprets the values and generates the appropriate intents related to the battery state. It will shut down the device when the battery is critically low.

Before getting into the details of the Android USB Battery Charging framework, it's important you understand what kind of information the Android kernel exports that is related to battery charging in the user space. The following snippet lists files and folders under /sys/class/power_supply using the ADB shell of a Samsung Grand mobile:

```
shell@android:/sys/class/power_supply $ ls
ac
battery
bcm59056_charger
fuelgauge
usb
shell@android:/sys/class/power_supply $

shell@android:/sys/class/power_supply/battery $ ls
batt_lp_charging
batt_read_adj_soc
batt_read_raw_soc
batt_reset_soc
batt_temp_adc
batt_temp_adc_aver
batt_temp_aver
batt_type
capacity
capacity_level
device
health
model_name
power
present
status
subsystem
technology
temp
type
uevent
voltage_now
shell@android:/sys/class/power_supply/battery $
```

Few of the file entries listed here are specific to the vendor, and this section focuses only on the entries that the Android framework uses. Internally, the Android framework reads these files using a JNI implementation (frameworks/base/services/jni/com_android_server_BatteryService. cpp) and stores them internally for sharing with other applications. In the following section, you'll explore how a Battery Manager and Battery Service, as represented in Figure A-6, generate battery charging-related intents. Android Battery Charger framework uses the following intents to pass on the status of battery charging.

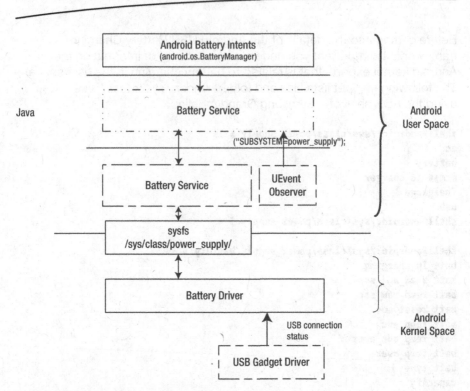

Figure A-6. Illustrates the Android Battery Manager architecture when plugged in to a USB power source

android.intent.action.BATTERY_CHANGED

This intent is generated to indicate that some of the battery-related information has changed and any interested receiver has to recalculate. The intent bundles the following extra data for the receiver, which can be used to develop advanced battery applications:

```
STATUS - The status field holds one of the following values:
            - BATTERY_STATUS_UNKNOWN = 1;
      - BATTERY_STATUS_CHARGING = 2;
            - BATTERY_STATUS_DISCHARGING = 3;
            - BATTERY_STATUS_NOT_CHARGING = 4;
            - BATTERY_STATUS_FULL = 5;
HEALTH - The health field holds one of the following values:
            - BATTERY_HEALTH_UNKNOWN = 1;
            - BATTERY_HEALTH_GOOD = 2;
            - BATTERY_HEALTH_OVERHEAT = 3;
            - BATTERY_HEALTH_DEAD = 4;
            - BATTERY_HEALTH_OVER_VOLTAGE = 5;
```

```
        - BATTERY_HEALTH_UNSPECIFIED_FAILURE = 6;
        - BATTERY_HEALTH_COLD = 7;
```
PRESENT - The present field indicates the presence of the battery.
LEVEL - The level field indicates current battery level.
SCALE - The scale field indicates the maximum battery level, indicated
        as BATTERY_SCALE = 100 in BatteryService.java.
ICON_SMALL - The icon field hold the resource id of the battery icon
             based on the current battery status retreived by
             getIconLocked in BatteryService.java
PLUGGED - The plugged field indicates the type of power source and the
          value could be one of the following:
          /** Power source is an AC charger. */
          - BATTERY_PLUGGED_AC = 1;
          /** Power source is a USB port. */
          - BATTERY_PLUGGED_USB = 2;
          /** Power source is wireless. */
          - BATTERY_PLUGGED_WIRELESS = 4;
VOLTAGE - The voltage field indicates current battery voltage in
          Millivolts.
TEMPERATURE - The temperature field indicates current battery
               temperature in tenths of a degree Centigrade.
TECHNOLOGY - The technology field specifices the technology that battery is
made of.
INVALID_CHARGER - When the charge is unsupported, the charger variable is
set to non-zero numeral.
```

An important point to note about this intent is a protected intent can be sent only by the system. This intent cannot be received through manifest declarations and has to be explicitly registered.

## android.intent.action.BATTERY_LOW

This intent is generated by the Android Battery framework to indicate that the device has reached a low battery level. This intent can be sent only by the system and is a protected intent.

## android.intent.action.BATTERY_OKAY

This intent is generated by the Android Battery framework to indicate that the device has recovered from a low battery level and is now OK. This intent can be sent only by the system and is a protected intent.

## android.intent.action.ACTION_POWER_CONNECTED

This intent is generated by the Android Battery framework when an external power source is connected to the system. Any application registered for this intent will be woken up and this protected intent can be sent only by the system.
```

android.intent.action.ACTION_POWER_DISCONNECTED

This intent is generated by the Android Battery framework when an external power source is disconnected from the system. Any application registered for this intent will be woken up, and this protected intent can be sent only by the system.

Android Battery Framework Design

Having learned about the different intents related to Android Battery framework, you're ready to explore how these intents are generated and sent to applications that are registered for these battery notifications. Figure A-7 illustrates the sequence of operations for how a battery framework registers to an Android platform until the intent generation.

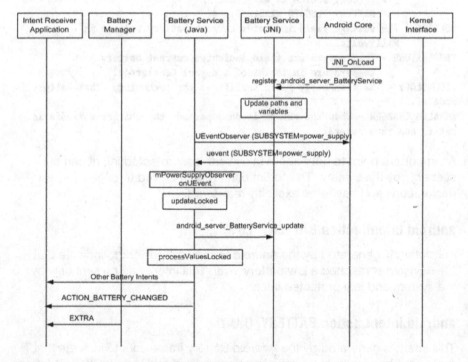

Figure A-7. The control flow of the Battery Service framework

The core part of the Android Battery framework is the Battery Service, which is extended using Battery Manager with battery-related information for an application. The Battery Service starts when the system loads up with the JNI_OnLoad function. That function registers different frameworks, including the Battery Service using the register_android_server_BatteryService function, as illustrated in Figure A-8.

The Battery Service Java implementation starts observing for SUBSYSTEM=power_supply uevents from the battery kernel driver. When the string is matched by the UEventObserver, the Battery Service framework starts reading the sysfs entries using the JNI function android_server_ BatteryService_update. The read values are compared with the previously read values, which were stored internally within the Battery Service framework. If the read value is different from the stored value, then the Battery Service framework generates appropriate intents to communicate the battery status to other Android frameworks.

From the sequence diagram Figure A-7, you can now see that the Battery Manager class acts as a holder for the ACTION_BATTERY_CHANGED Intents' extras. When applications receive the ACTION_BATTERY_CHANGED intent, they can retrieve the additional data using the getIntExtra method, with constants defined in the Battery Manager, as shown here:

```
int plugged = intent.getIntExtra(BatteryManager.EXTRA_PLUGGED, 0);
```

 DID YOU KNOW?

Here are a few interesting change lists extracted from the Battery Service framework's history:

Fix a deadlock involving Battery Service (Ibf8ab13224f204a9857825265e864f93583bce8e)

The PowerManager may call into the Battery Service while holding its locks. You need to be careful that the Battery Service doesn't call into other services, particularly the Activity Manager, while holding its own locks.

Change-Id: Ibf8ab13224f204a9857825265e864f93583bce8e

This is a very recent fix, and if you are developing a battery application for older Android versions like Gingerbread, you may be interested in this defect.

Shut down when capacity is 0% with no charging or when battery is dead.

The Android framework does not shut down when battery capacity is 0% and a charger is attached (USB or AC). This handling is incomplete since a charger might very well be attached, but the charging has stopped because the USB is suspended or the charging algorithm has stopped because of battery safety handling. Also, shutdown may occur when the battery is reported as "dead." This might still happen, although the device may be currently charging.

Change-Id: If328260ebf4d38f912e4d2fad204431cbb19c993

This change list can provide an idea of how to manage the battery status information and control system shutdown. This was reverted and modified through change list I1e6590611af43812f1bac223dd31570d1d90cfc5.

Now that you have an understanding of the internals of the Android Battery framework, it's time to explore how to use this information to develop advanced battery applications. The following section provides two example applications demonstrating how to:

- Access the battery driver system information by bypassing the Android Battery framework.

- Use the Android Battery framework intent to detect when the battery is full.

Sample 1: Battery Status Explorer

The purpose of this example is to demonstrate how an application can bypass the Android Battery framework and collect information about the battery's status directly from the files exported by the Android battery driver.

Design and Flo

The Android kernel battery driver exports battery information through files mounted in the /sys/class/power_supply folder. The Android Battery framework reads those files and broadcasts the contents as part of the battery intents. However, an application developer can bypass this framework and directly read the system files to gain additional information about the battery status.

The application starts by setting up the default directory to /sys/class/power_supply/battery/, which needs to be listed as shown here:

```
public class MainActivity extends Activity {

    private File f= new File("/sys/class/power_supply/battery/");
    private String []directory;
    private String start = "/sys/class/power_supply/battery/";
```

The application uses BaseExpandableListAdapter to list the file and the contents on a click event, as shown here:

```
ExpandableListView myview = (ExpandableListView)findViewById(R.
id.expandableListView1);
myview.setOnChildClickListener(new ExpandableListView.OnChildClickListener() {

    @Override
    public boolean onChildClick(ExpandableListView parent, View v,
                int groupPosition, int childPosition, long id) {

--cut--
```

```
            File myfile = new File(start + directory[groupPosition]);
            if(myfile.exists()) {
                    if (myfile.isDirectory()) {
--cut--
                            adp.notifyDataSetChanged();

--cut--                                 }
            }
            else
                    return false;
--cut--
adp = new myAdapter(getBaseContext(), directory, start);
myview.setAdapter(adp);
```

The snapshot in Figure A-8 shows the application list /sys/class/power_
supply/battery folder along with its contents.

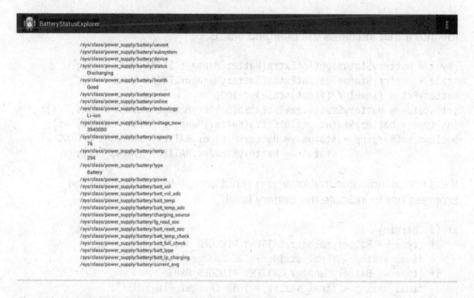

Figure A-8. Snapshot of Battery status explorer application

The complete code and project are available at http://www.apress.com/
9781430262084 and at https://git.techfugen.com/cgit/Android/apps/
git/batterystatusexplorer.git/. You can download the code and send
patches to add functionalities to the project.

Sample 2: Charging Completion Indicator

The purpose of this example is to demonstrate how an application can parse information from the ACTION_BATTERY_CHANGED intent and generate an alarm when charging is complete. The application also indicates the charging progress using a progress bar.

Design and Flow

As discussed in the initial sections of this appendix, if an application is interested in receiving the intent ACTION_BATTERY_CHANGED, it has to register rather than project the manifest file.

```
ifilter = new IntentFilter(Intent.ACTION_BATTERY_CHANGED);
batteryStatus = registerReceiver(null, ifilter);
```

After successful registration, you can extract the information passed over on the intent that indicates the charging status.

```
level = batteryStatus.getIntExtra(BatteryManager.EXTRA_LEVEL, -1);
scale = batteryStatus.getIntExtra(BatteryManager.EXTRA_SCALE, -1);
batteryPct = (level / (float)scale) * 100;
int status = batteryStatus.getIntExtra(BatteryManager.EXTRA_STATUS, -1);
int type = batteryStatus.getIntExtra(BatteryManager.EXTRA_PLUGGED, -1);
boolean isCharging = status == BatteryManager.BATTERY_STATUS_CHARGING ||
                     status == BatteryManager.BATTERY_STATUS_FULL;
```

If the status indicates that charging is not complete, you can set the progress bar to indicate the battery level.

```
if (isCharging) {
    if (type == BatteryManager.BATTERY_PLUGGED_AC)
        final_string = final_string + "AC Charger Plugged\n";
    if (type == BatteryManager.BATTERY_PLUGGED_USB)
        final_string = final_string + "USB Charger Plugged\n";
    textview.setText( final_string + "Battery % = " + batteryPct);
    if (progressbar.getProgress() <= 99) {
        progressbar.incrementProgressBy(1);

    } else {
        progressbar.setProgress((int)batteryPct);
    }
```

Once charging is complete and the battery is full, you can then play a tone for a brief period.

```
} else {
    textview.setText(final_string + "Battery % = " + batteryPct);
    progressbar.setProgress((int)batteryPct);
    genTone();
    if (temp < 10) {
        if ((temp & 1) == 1)
            audioTrack.play();
        else
            audioTrack.stop();
        temp++;
    }
}

}
```

This application indicates when to plug in a phone when charging and to switch off the power source when the battery is fully charged. The complete code and project are available at http://www.apress.com/9781430262084 and at https://git.techfugen.com/cgit/Android/apps/git/charging completeindicator.git/. Figure A-9 provides a snapshot of the application.

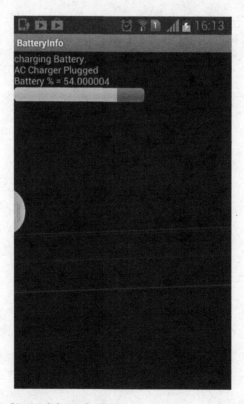

Figure A-9. Snapshot of batteryinfo application

Conclusion

USB as a power source has come a long way and has matured through formal specifications like the USB-IF's *Battery Charging Specification*. This appendix explored the different charger types in laymen terms and then matched those devices with battery specification requirements. This appendix also explored the charging frameworks inside Android and included detailed examples.

Let's not forget also to explore a recent development in the evolution of USB-based charging, known as "USB power delivery." The power delivery specification is designed to deliver increased power levels and relax power direction, which means either the host or device can supply power and supportive negotiating power is required. You can find more detailed information on power delivery on the USB organization's website at http://www.usb.org/developers/powerdelivery/.

Using libusb in Android

What you will learn:

- Overview of libusbhost
- USB-Serial Driver Using libusb
- Building and Installing the Package
- Running the USB-Serial Application

Developers who have worked for USB development requirements or have conducted feasibility studies should definitely have encountered the ubiquitous USB software library or the driver called libusb. Be it Windows, Linux, or Mac, a libusb driver is available on all of these leading operating systems and provides a generic interface in order to access and manage USB devices that are connected to the system. On Linux, libusb is referred to as the user space driver, which accesses the USB devices through the device files exported by the usb-core driver in the Linux kernel. Android with Linux kernel uses similar designs to manage USB devices connected to Android power devices when acting in USB host mode.

The Android platform introduced USB host mode support in the Honeycomb version by providing host APIs, as described in Chapter 1, "Getting Started: The Android USB Framework." This, however, was improved upon in the Ice Cream Sandwich version of Android, at which point the complete system that is available today was put in place. Android introduced a new library, called libusbhost, which is a thinner version of libusb as the generic user space driver for USB devices in the Android platform. The latest version of the Android framework also includes libusb and libusb-compat library sources.

This appendix explores the new library, libusbhost, in brief and explains how USB host APIs use it for interacting with USB devices. In the following sections, the appendix explains how to develop custom Android frameworks using libusb for Android with an example. This example explains how to develop JNI and aJava class, and includes a sample applications to fit to the proprietary requirements using Cypress USB-serial development kits.

Overview of libusbhost

Linux kernel exposes USB devices connected to the system to the user space through its device file system, which then enables user space applications to manage the devices. Using this feature, the generic user space library libusb evolved to manage the USB devices connected to the Linux kernel from the user space. This open source library gives applications easy access to USB devices with APIs. They allow open/close communication with USB devices, perform control/data transfers, and even contain a USB device reset.

There are two versions of the libusb APIs:

> libusb-0.1: This is the original version of libusb; it's now deprecated.

> libusb-1.0: This is the current version, with many new features when compared to the legacy version, and is recommended for new development.

There is also a compatibility library called libusb-compat-0.1.5 that provides legacy API compatibility for the current version of libusb, allowing older applications to have API compatibility. Additional information about libusb can be found from its official web site at www.libusb.org.

The Android framework includes the current version of libusb and libusb-compact in the following directories, respectively: external/libusb/ and external/libusb-compat/. Interestingly, the Android USB framework does not use both of these libraries, but brings in a thinner user space library called libusbhost that's used for managing USB devices connected to an Android powered device. The implementation of libusbhost is available in the system/core/libusbhost/ directory. Figure B-1 provides a top-level architectural view of the libusbhost framework.

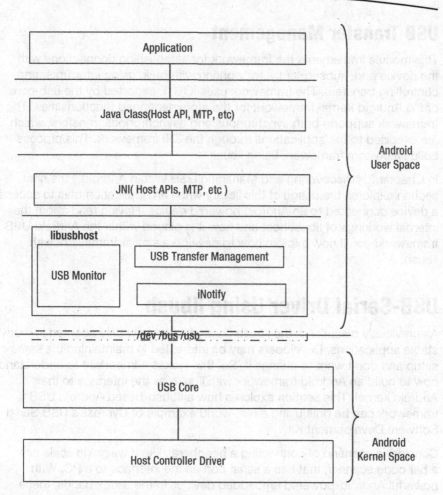

Figure B-1. *The internals of libusbhost and their placement in an Android framework*

As illustrated in Figure B-1, libusbhost is a simple implementation, providing access to USB devices enumerated by the usb-core of the Linux kernel. Though the library is implemented in a single file (system/core/libusbhost/usbhost.c), the library is divided into possible functional blocks to better represent the simplicity of the library.

USB Monitor

This module implements the addition and removal of USB devices using the iNotify framework. The addition and removal information is passed through the callbacks that are registered when the JNI framework starts monitoring USB activity.

USB Transfer Management

This module implements the framework for establishing connections with the device and, subsequently, for working with bulk, using interrupts, and controlling transfers. The framework uses IOCTL exported by the usb-core of the Android kernel framework for the aforementioned functionalities. The framework supports both synchronous and asynchronous transfers, which are exported to the applications through the JNI framework. This process builds a custom framework using libusb.

In Chapter 2, "Discovering and Managing USB Within Android," the host section explores the usage of this library when an application tries to access a device connected to an Android powered device. Having read about the internal workings of libusbhost and how it is placed within the Android USB framework, you'll now explore how to develop a similar framework with libusb.

USB-Serial Driver Using libusb

As previously discussed, the libusb library has been widely adapted in many stable applications. Developers may be interested in maintaining the same setup and don't want to change it. So, this makes it important to understand how to build an Android framework with libusb as the interface to the Android kernel. This section explores how a libusb-based Android USB framework can be built using a real-world example of Cypress's USB Serial Software Development Kit.

Consider a scenario of connecting a peripheral, like a weighing scale or a bar code scanner, that has a serial port as the interface to a PC. With powerful Android-powered embedded devices in the user's hands, these peripherals need to support these devices. With Android devices providing only a USB port, a USB-serial converter is an ideal solution to enable these devices to connect. Figure B-2 illustrates a setup of connecting a peripheral device, with a USB-serial converter, to an Android-powered device with USB host support.

Figure B-2. A typical setup for connecting a weighing scale to an Android device

To understand this setup, you'll use the USB-to-serial converter of a Cypress semiconductor: the USB-serial bridge controller. Cypress's USB-serial bridge controller is a full-speed USB controller that provides configurable serial channels that allow users to select UART, I2C, or SPI instead of the USB interface. You can find more about this chip on Cypress's web site at http://www.cypress.com/?id=4858&tabID=82672. Cypress also provides a complete library and driver stack for USB-serial bridge controller devices in order to facilitate integration of USB interfaces into an embedded application. The Software Development Kit (SDK) provides configuration tools, libraries, and drivers, including an Android-based driver application solution. This solution uses libusb as the base library to interface with the serial bridge controller, and you can download the driver and application from http://www.cypress.com/?rID=83110.

The Android package contains a library based on libusb 1.0.9, a JNI interface, a Java class, and an application that communicates to the serial bridge controller, as shown in Figure B-3.

Figure B-3. The code base of Cypress's Android serial driver

Figure B-4 illustrates how the libusb-based Android framework of the Cypress USB-serial bridge fits into the Android USB framework architecture.

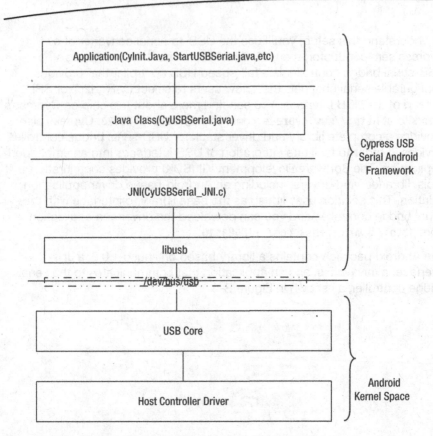

Figure B-4. The internals of Cypress's USB-serial Android framework

Building and Installing the Package

Now that you have a basic understanding of the package contents, this section explores how to build and install the package in an Android-powered device with USB host support. To build the package, you should have the latest Android SDK and the Android NDK toolsets, which are available from the http://developer.android.com/sdk/index.html web site. After these toolsets are succesfully installed, open the Eclipse tool available in the Android SDK and import the project workspace. The imported workspace will look like Figure B-3. To configure NDK and set the NDK tool location, select the Project Properties ➤ Builder ➤ NDK_Builder ➤ Edit option, as shown in Figure B-5.

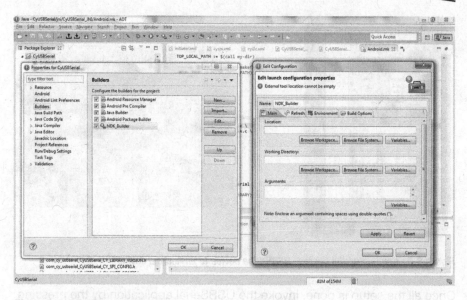

Figure B-5. The Setup of NDK

After successfully configuring NDK in the Eclipse environment, you should build the package to generate two binaries: the Android application (./bin/CyUSBSerial.apk) and the Cypress USB-serial library (./obj/local/armeabi/libCyUSBSerial.so).

Once the binaries are built, it is important to load the Android device that the USB-serial bridge device is to be connected to. Use the following code to install the library and the application:

```
#adb push ./obj/local/armeabi/libCyUSBSerial.so /data/local/tmp
#adb install CyUSBSerial.apk
```

You can also refer to the README.txt file, which is part of this package, for additional information on the setup and building procedures.

Running the USB-Serial Application

In the test setup, the Cypress's USB-serial bridge device is connected to a rooted Samsung Tab2 Android device, illustrated in Figure B-6. Since this is a custom framework, it is important that the Android device be rooted, thus allowing the addition of new libraries. It is also important to change the permission of the USB-serial bridge device's entry created in /dev/bus/usb/* so that the application can open, close, or send data to the serial bridge device.

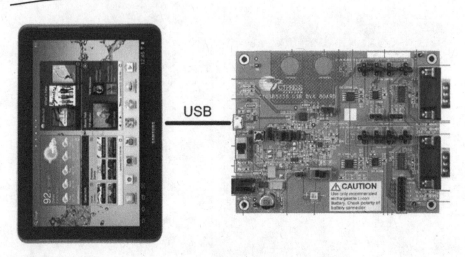

Figure B-6. Connecting the Cypress USBBridge device to an Android device

Once all the setup is done, invoke the USBSerial application by the pressing the icon created for the application. Figure B-7 provides a snapshot of the initial screen of the application. Enter the VID and PID of Cypress's USB-serial bridge device, as shown in Figure B-7.

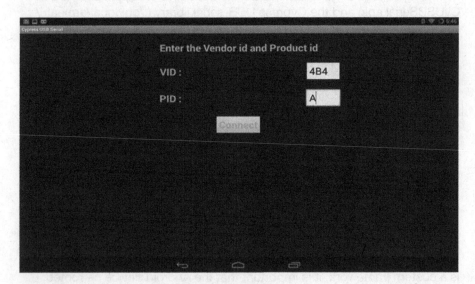

Figure B-7. Initial screen of the USBSerial bridge application

Now, when you click Connect, the application searches for the device using the libusb library. Then you may begin the USBSerial activity, as shown here:

```
deviceCount = CyUSBSerial.getDeviceInfoVIDPID(deviceNumber,
    deviceInfoA, cyVIDPID, infoListSize);
if (deviceCount > 0) {
    Intent ret = new Intent(CyInit.this, StartUSBSerial.class);
    startActivity(ret);
    finish();
}
```

This hand-over takes the application to a new interface, as shown in Figure B-8.

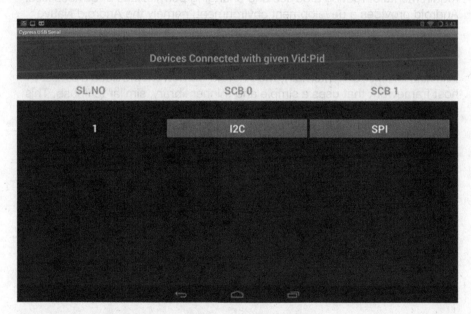

Figure B-8. The initial screen of the USBSerial bridge application

The next step in the process is to choose which serial interface to use in order to communicate with the serial device from the available interface, such as I2C or SPI. Based on the interface selection, the application starts the equivalent service, as shown:

```
String text = b.getText().toString();
if(text.equals("SPI"))
{
    Intent ret = new Intent(StartUSBSerial.this, SpiConfig.class);
    startActivity(ret);
```

```
    finish();
}
else if(text.equals("I2C"))
{
    Intent ret = new Intent(StartUSBSerial.this, I2CConfig.class);
    startActivity(ret);
    finish();
}
```

This application provided a brief overview of how to build a custom Android USB framework based on the libusb library. Such a custom setup can be very useful in development mode and when providing proprietary API interfaces. On the contrary, this kind of custom setup brings additional requirements of rooting a device and changing permissions of devices files. Android provides a development environment, namely the Android Native Development Kit (NDK), which allows developers to build such libraries and integrate the Android framework. To study more about how to build an application using NDK, refer to http://developer.android.com/tools/sdk/ndk/index.html. Internally, the Android framework provides a similar host framework that uses a simple and thinner library, similar to libusb. This was explained in Chapter 2 in detail, which provided an example of how to communicate with a USB device.

Index

■ A

ADB daemon, 131–133
Android accessory audio dock, 118
Android Accessory Development
    Kit (ADK), 80
Android battery charging
    battery framework design
        control flow, 150
        JNI_OnLoad function, 150
        Powermanager, 151
    battery service, 146
        android.intent.action., 148
        architecture, plug in, 148
        JNI implementation, 147
        snippet files and folders, 147
Android Debug Bridge (ADB)
    architecture
        adb_client.c file, 133
        ADB daemon, 133
        backup command, 136–137
        building blocks, Android
          powered device, 132
        commandline.c file, 133
        file execution, 133
        JDWP process, 135
    definition, 125
    protocol
        client–server
          communication, 129
        command messages, 130
        information flow, 131
        strings of ASCII
          characters, 130
        TCP transport, 129
        USB transport, 129

setup
    adb shell command, 126
    DDMS tool, 126
    Linux, 128
    terminal and DDMS, 126
    Windows, 127
    three key components, 125–126
Android Open Accessory (AOA)
    framework, 88
    AOA communication, 92
    AOA device detection, 90
    architecture of, 89
    in HID registration and
        communication process, 93
    NFC reader and NFC tag, 95
        CyFX3_AOA_NFC
          application, 98
        sequence of activities, 96
        setup, 96
    responder implementation, 88
Android Open Accessory (AOA)
    protocol, 79–80
    accessory mode, 81–82
    ACCESSORY_START, 84
    audio USB interface, 81
    control request, 83
    HID feature, 81, 83
    string information request, 85
    with Android-powered
        devices, 79
Android USB, 1
    CDD definition, 2
    CDD requirements, 2
        USB accessory mode, 4
        USB device mode, 2, 4
        USB host mode, 3, 5

Android USB (*cont.*)
  framework architecture, 7–8
    android.hardware.usb
      package, 9
    class drivers, 8
    infrastructure, 9, 11
    kernel file system, 11
    libusbhost, 11
    USB functions, 9
    USB host mode class, 8, 11
    USB service, 11
  Media Transfer Protocol
    (MTP), 6
  packages, 12
    accessory device, 12
    android.hardware.usb
      package, 12
    android.mtp class, 14
    UsbDevice, 13
    UsbDeviceConnection, 13
    UsbEndpoint, 14
    UsbInterface, 13
    UsbManager, 13
    UsbRequest, 14
Android USB management, 17
  device management, 18
  device manager (*see* USB
    Device management)
  host management, 18
  host manager, 27
    ACTION_USB_DEVICE_
      DETACHED intent, 32
    design and flow, 33
    device communication, 31
    device discovery, 29
    framework, 29
    inotify system, 32
    JNI-level, 28
    USB_DEVICE_ATTACHED
      intent, 33
    UsbRequest
      framework, 28
  USB servicebuilding
    blocks, 20
  USB service framework, 19

B

Bulk-Only Transport (BOT)
  protocol, 39, 42

C

Class drivers, 8
Command block wrapper (CBW), 41
Command Status Wrapper (CSW), 41
Cypress
  Android serial driver, 161
  USBBridge device, 164
  USB-serial Android
    framework, 162
  USBSerial bridge
    application, 164–166
Cypress FX3, 118

D, E, F, G

Dalvik Debug Monitor Server
  (DDMS) debugging tool, 126
Digital-to-analog converter (DAC), 119

H, I

HID physical descriptor, 87
HID report descriptor, 87
Human Interface Devices (HIDs), 85

J, K

Java Debug Wire Protocol (JDWP)
  process, 135

L

libusb
  APIs, 158
  Cypress
    Android serial driver, 161
    USBBridge device, 164
    USB-serial Android
      framework, 162
    USBSerial bridge
      application, 164–166

definition, 157
NDK setup, 162–163
peripheral device, 160
USB-Serial Driver, 160
libusbhost
architectural view, 158–159
overview of, 158
Linux, 128

M

Media Transfer Protocol
(MTP), 6–7, 38, 49
application selection, 66
CameraBrowser application, 67
communication model, 50
host/initiator framework, 58
android.mtp Package APIs, 58
architechture, 59
command/response
sequence, 61
discovering and managing, 60
implementation, 6
interface and endpoint
decriptors, 50
operation-data-response
model, 49
responder enumeration, 53
responder framework, 53
command/response
sequence, 56
MTPDatabase class, 55
MTPDataPacket class, 55
MTPEventPacket class, 55
MTPRequestPacket class, 55
MTPResponsePacket class, 55
MTPServer class, 54
StorageBrowser and
ObjectBrowser scan, 67
transport-agnostic protocol, 50
to UMS, 62
MTP host mode, 9

N, O, P, Q

Near field communication (NFC), 95

R, S

Remote Network Driver Interface
Specification (RNDIS), 69
architechture, 72
CDC data interface, 73
definition, 71
interface descriptor, 73

T

Terminal, 104

U, V, W, X, Y, Z

USB
monitor, 159
transfer management, 160
USB accessory, 79
USB audio, 101
analog audio, 102
android-powered devices, 102
Android USB audio, 105
architechtural view, 106
DEVICE_OUT_USB_
ACCESSORY, 108
DEVICE_OUT_USB_
DEVICE, 108
frameworks, 107
USB device audio (see USB
device audio)
USB host audio (see USB
host audio)
class specification, 102
host audio, 102
USB charger
Android battery charging (see
Android battery charging)
battery specification
accessory charger
adapter (ACA), 144
Charging downstream
port (CDP), 143
dedicated downstream
port (DCP), 144
downstream port, 142

USB charger (*cont.*)
    standard downstream
      port (SDP), 143
    upstream port, 142
  battery status explorer, 152
  charging completion
    indicator, 154
  types
    charging dock, 141
    personal computer, 141
    wall charger, 140
UsbDebuggingManager
    device, 133
USB device audio
  accessory mode, 113, 116
  android accessory audio
    dock, 118
  architecture, 114–115
  configuration, 117–118
  Cypress FX3, 118
  feature, 113
  product ID, 114
  vendor-defined control, 116
USB Device management
  Android Gadget Driver uevents
    KOBJ_CHANGE action, 25
    mode functions, 26
    state changes, 25
    uevent mechanism, 24
    USB_STATE format, 24
  framework, 21
  function configuration
    actions class, 22
    Android Init language, 22
    parameters, 23
UsbDeviceManager
    device, 133
USB host audio, 102
  architecture, 110
  enumeration, 111
  framework, 112
  intent broadcast snapshot of, 112

  soundcard snapshot of, 111
  USB_AUDIO_DEVICE_PLUG
    intent, 109
USB Human Interface Device (HID)
  class specification, 85
  descriptor tree, 86
  physical descriptor, 87
  report descriptor, 87
  setup, 85
USB Mass Storage (UMS), 38
  BOT protocol, 39
  class specification, 39
  command block wrapper, 41
  command status wrapper, 41
  device framework, 43
    class implementation of, 44
    host architechture, 48
    kernal driver
      implementation, 44
    MMC driver, 45
  interface and endpoints
    descriptors, 40
  MountService, 46
USB storage, 37
USB technology. *See* USB charger
USB tethering, 69–70
  Remote Network Driver Interface
    Specification (RNDIS)
    architechture, 71
    CDC data interface, 73
    definition, 71
    interface descriptor, 72
  reverse tethering, 76
    device setup, 77
    host setup, 77
  USB tethering framework, 74
    activity diagram, 76
    architechture, 75
    setUSBTethering interface
      function, 75
    TetherSettings.java, 75
    updateUsbState, 75

Get the eBook for o

This Apress title will prove so indispensible that you'l
you everywhere, which is why we are offering the eE
only $10 if you have already purchased the print boo

Convenient and fully searchable, the PDF version en
find and copy code—or perform examples by quickly
instructions and   applications. The MOBI format is ide
while the ePUB can be utilized on a variety of mobile c

Go to www.apress.com/promo/tendollars to purchase
eBook.

Apress®
THE EXPERT'S VOICE™